FREEDOM

Ours For The Asking

The author asserts her moral rights over this work under the terms of Section 96 of the Copyright Act of 1994 (New Zealand.) All rights reserved. No part of this publication may be produced or transmitted in any form or by any means, electronic, or mechanical, including photocopying, recording, or information storage and retrieval systems, without permission in writing from the copyright holder.

© Jocelynne Jones
2014

ISBN 978-0-9941045-3-3 (paperback)
ISBN 978-0-9941045-5-7 (kindle)

The Little Red Hen Community Press
Tauranga
Aotearoa

ABOUT THE AUTHOR

Jocelynne Jones is the pen-name of a writer living in New Zealand. Retired, with two grownup offspring and a granddaughter, she is a quiet-living family person whose writing has, up until the age of ebooks, been little more than a hobby. With the establishment of 'indie publishers' Jocelynne has found an outlet for a passion that was hitherto stifled by previous publishing systems.

Other titles by the same author are:

'Whiskey Rose' – the story of a family faced with the constraints of caring for an elderly relative.
'Lucifer's Story' – a fantasy tale of good-over-evil, which envisions the end of evil forever. It is set in a parallel universe called Eternity.
'Guarding My Angel' – a drama based on the author's autobiography.

To Jenny.

With grateful thanks, as always!

FREEDOM

Ours For The Asking

Jocelynne Jones

CONTENTS

INTRODUCTION 1

PART ONE 4

WHY FREEDOM? 5
FREEDOM IN NATURE 10
RELEASE OF THE MIND 21
IT CAN HAPPEN TO YOU 31
OPENING OUT A WAY 42
A CORNER TURNED 49
SOME PROBLEMS OVERCOME 55
    Communication 56
    Getting on with other people 58
    Controlling thought processes 61
    Attaining peace of mind 63
    The effects of negative thought 65
    Coping with mood fluctuations 68
    Getting a grip on anger 70
    Release from jealousy 72
    Blame, guilt and temptation 73
    The importance of trust 77
    The use of willpower 78
    Loneliness and insecurity 82
    Taking the easy way out 84
    Everyday needs and feelings 86
    Finding our niche in life 88

- Physical contact and love 92
- Marriage 95
- The role of parenthood 98
- The complexity of youth 102
- Encroaching old age 107
- Chronic, debilitating and terminal illness..................110
- Addictions 112
- Hobbies and entertainment 116
- Daily supply 117

PIECES IN A JIGSAW..121
THE PRICE TO PAY 129

PART TWO 134
CHANNELLING THE SPIRIT 135
A SEPARATE STATE 140
VARIATIONS ON A THEME 149
OUT OF DARKNESS 154
A POINT OF NO RETURN 159
A SECOND CHANCE 163
AS YOU SOW...175
SAY ONE FOR ME 179
AND THE GREATEST OF THESE… 184
A MOVE IS AFOOT 189
UNIVERSAL GATHERING 196

INTRODUCTION

The world of today is full of problems, but none is so close to home as our lack of understanding about who we are.

Not many people can honestly say they're happy being themselves or living the lives that they lead. Many feel something's lacking in their lives but can't pinpoint what it is, causing in them a sense of isolation.

You could say we're like sole inhabitants of self-made fortresses, living in lonely isolation. We may not even be consciously aware of it or we're reluctant to admit it, but nevertheless it's true. It seems to be a consequence of living in today's Western 'civilised' society, and not many of us are able to avoid it.

Could this also apply to you? Have you in one way or other isolated *yourself* from the world?

Do you even care who you are and why you're here? You: that thinking, feeling unique inhabitant whose true identity, for the moment, seems to be concealed?

Maybe you're simply tired of being you; or rather you are tired of being dragged at breakneck speed through life, when a big part of you is crying out for recognition and freedom.

Do you wish you could barricade your personal fortress against the outside world, because modern day values seem to go against the grain; that is, against *your* grain.

Yet, you're somehow persuaded the status quo is right and that you must be strange if you think differently?

If these words ring true, and cause you to feel annoyed because there is nothing you can do about it, then cast your mind over this for a moment:

Imagine life – that is, life in general rather than your own personal life – as an abstract painting. To some, it is just a colourful but empty splurge of paint on canvas; to others it has great depth and beauty.

People who see only the 'splurge' are those who exist in the material world; the meaning of life is of little interest to them. Those who see the depth in the painting have broken through their worldliness, this veneer we have wrapped around life, and are now contentedly living their lives to the full.

Yet there are others who are tired of looking only at the splurge, and sense that there's more to the painting than meets the eye. Only, not knowing what it is or what to do about it, they become disillusioned.

It is my belief that if you find yourself questioning the splurge, if you want to understand it but don't know how to, then something deep inside you has indeed recognised there is more to your life. You are disillusioned right now because you don't know what it is, or what to do in order to move forward.

...Is this true?

Does the purpose of your life interest you?

Are you even driven crazy for want of answers?

If the response here is 'yes', then what's contained in this book might just strike home and provide the answers; or at least, some of them.

Let me tell you why I think it could help.

Some years ago I was also driven crazy for the need of answers. I had been playing out ordinary humdrum roles since childhood, and was established in a meaningless groove that left me feeling I had no identity of my own. I sank into a state of deep depression, losing all sense of identity, direction and freedom.

As a result, I retreated to the fortress of my own mind.

Then quite by chance I stumbled across something that gave every indication it was the answer – for me, anyway. Yet it was a long time before I could settle down and accept it; so great had been my dilemma beforehand. But after years of putting my discovery into practice, I now know that it *is* the answer. As a result, my whole outlook on life has changed.

It was like waking from a vivid nightmare to find, with utter relief, that it had only been a dream.

I am still playing out ordinary roles, but the difference now is that I'm at peace with my situation, because I'm also a free individual in my own right.

This book won't take long to read and is reasonably down to earth. It addresses the sort of problems and situations we're likely to encounter each day, but with some tried and now trusted remedies.

The theories contained within it offer a viable solution to many personal and universal problems. They can inspire peace, harmony and freedom in all who are willing to give it a try.

At very least I hope my words make the reader think.

So, if peace, harmony and freedom are your concept of 'life,' why don't *you* give the book a try?

PART ONE

WHY FREEDOM?

What do we mean by 'freedom'?

It's a word that's often bandied about, and yet true freedom always seems illusive.

Let's see what the dictionary says.

Here's one definition: 'State of being free; release from slavery, imprisonment, etc; exemption, frankness; absence of restraint.' Do any of these terms match your own way of thinking?

The word 'freedom' means different things to different people; some meanings more obvious than others, and yet all are significant in their own right.

Any person whose home is in a war zone or a country under military rule, may crave freedom from oppression. Someone who has lived in abject poverty or ill health all their life would crave release from such trying limitations. Whether a partner in an unhappy marriage, a bedridden pensioner, a young person hooked on drugs; someone with a dependent relative on their hands, or maybe just Mr or Ms Anybody bogged down in the tedium of day-to-day life, we each have something in common: the desire to be free.

No matter who we are, where we happen to live, and what our situation might be, at some time during our lives we all long for a sense of freedom.

Why, then, is freedom so important to us? Why, if we haven't got it, do we feel deprived of our rights? It's not as though we all long for the same kind of freedom. What appears to be imprisonment to some of us may seem like freedom to others.

For example: a lonely single woman, living on her own in a flat with a regular nine-to-five job, might gaze with envy on a married woman in a seemingly secure and happy relationship with her partner, her children and her home. But if we looked more closely we might find that the married woman longs to be free of her responsibilities, and may be envious of the single woman's independence.

It's the 'grass is greener on the other side of the hill' syndrome. Why doesn't the 'grass' appear green on our own side when others may look longingly at it?

Often we desire something we haven't got, but go on to find we're dissatisfied even after we've acquired it. This doesn't only apply to material things – better job, bigger house, flashier car, latest home entertainment centre – and all the other things we strive to attain and on which we place so much importance. These days questions of human rights and democracy are very much to the fore: freedom of speech; freedom of the press; freedom of choice; freedom for minority, cultural and ethnic groups; for women and gay people; for the individual, whoever he or she might be; even the freedom to be alone when we so desire. It's all freedom.

We are look to others to provide our freedom. In some instances we even expect it as entitlement – from our governments, our communities and our families. Often we're restless or dissatisfied with what we've got, and aspire to something different; to something better: to something else. We look back to the good old days or think ahead to better times; but all we can see is the confinement of the present. Does this sound familiar?

Some people are lucky. They seem able to achieve a certain amount of freedom during their lifetime. In any situation which begins to grind, they have the freedom to move on and keep moving on. But even so, is that real freedom? Are they also free of worries and fears within their own minds?

And how about people in a situation which cannot be altered without major upheaval and upset?

What do they do? What if the war never ends, the old man is bedridden all his life, or the woman is unable to break free of her shackles?

What if there is no let-up in the bickering between husband and wife?

When ordinary people are unable to break free of the rat race, what do *they* do; or rather, what do *we* do? In one way or another, this involves most of us. If nobody else is willing or able to help us, what on earth can we do?

Over the years helpful suggestions have been offered by people who care and are anxious to see humankind find and make something of itself. They encourage us to do our own thing; to be pro-active, think positive and so on: all manner of self-help guidelines. But not too many people even know what 'their own thing' is.

Anyway, how can someone else, no matter how qualified or well-meaning, really know what's best for us individually? Other people cannot possibly perceive the aspirations of the soul, or what course our life is likely to run. Whether anguish and unrest is brought about by a pimply face, fear of the unknown, a sense of confinement or the death of a goldfish, to each of us it may be the most terrible thing in the world. Yet it remains comparatively unimportant to someone else.

Furthermore, when we each have a problem, do we even understand what the problem is, know what to do about it, or feel able to discuss it with other people?

Newspapers, magazines and television often try to persuade us to do something stimulating or cultivate a leisure pursuit. We're urged to take up a hobby, meet people, find a job, have a holiday, travel, buy on interest-free credit – all sorts of things that cost time and money we might not have, even if they do succeed in providing a welcome distraction.

However, the benefits of such distractions themselves are short-lived.

Sooner or later we still have to go back home; back to the conflict in our own minds. At some stage in every 24 hours we have to return to our fears, doubts and worries; not forgetting the long nights with only our thoughts for company, when we sometimes sink to rock bottom.

What do we do then? Resort to tranquillisers? Take to drink or drugs? Or even, sad to say, commit suicide?

Unfortunately some do; but deep down inside we know that these are *not* the answer.

You might be thinking, after this depressing scenario, that there *is* no ready solution to the problems in our lives at the moment.

...But there is.

Oh yes, there most definitely is.

It would seem, though, that a great many Westerners are unaware of it.

You see, the search for freedom and the state of being I've described here were the pattern of my own outlook on life while I was immersed in that nightmare of mine. It was awful and it was real. At least, it seemed that way. While I was living out that dreary existence – I hesitate to call it 'life' – the whole scene was very real to me. Yet, just as a nightmare seems very real to the dreamer no matter how bizarre and unlikely it may be, and the moment the dreamer awakens he realises it was only a dream; so it was with me. The instant I awoke I clearly recognised, although I couldn't instantly comprehend, that it had all been like a bad dream.

Freedom is definitely ours for the asking. There's no cost or hard work involved; it's simplicity itself, and it can be 100% effective. Achieving it merely consists of each of us understanding and applying certain principles to the nature of our lives.

If this whets your appetite to know more about it, then please read on.

FREEDOM IN NATURE

The awakening from the nightmare we think of as life is the true meaning of freedom. However, it's not like taking a painkiller: one minute you have a headache, the next minute it's gone. A certain amount of insight and patience is required to bring this about. We need to take things one at a time, as though gradually climbing up a ladder.

This calls for a return to basics in order to work our way up each 'rung.'

Hopefully, in the process, we may be able to touch on thoughts and experiences that explain why people remain in their own, very personal nightmare.

So; back to those basics:

We are human beings: homo sapiens – the highest form of life on this planet, the most intelligent creatures on earth.

We can think for ourselves, have the capacity to invent and to create, are able to appreciate the beauties in life; even, so we are told, to choose our own destiny. We can work things out and make our own decisions.

Yes, we're human beings and we, as Westerners, are proud of the fact.

Wait just a minute, though; something doesn't ring true. What is there to be proud of, really? If Westerners are so intelligent, then why do our complicated lives appear to be in such a mess – and not only our own lives, but seemingly the lives of others, too?

It doesn't make any difference whether we're wealthy or not, adult or not, intellectual or not. It doesn't matter what culture or religion we belong to; we're all susceptible to having things go wrong, and are equally capable of making mistakes. This is borne out both by the regularity with which life feels like a nightmare and because there is so much strife in the world. And not just in the world at large, but also in our own homes and lives – and in the dark recesses of our own minds.

Ah, that could be it: our minds. It harks back to how we think and feel about things. Perhaps it would help if we didn't even have thinking minds. Picture what this world would be like if human beings weren't here at all.

Imagine you're standing at the top of a hill with a view – not one of a seething, sprawling city, but overlooking the gentle, peaceful countryside with no sign of humanity. What do you see?

Nothing, you might say; but take a closer look. Do you see the birds casually riding the thermals, or a rabbit bobbing across open ground to disappear into the bush? Look even closer and you may be able to see the perfectly formed blossom on the trees, or the delicate spider's web suspended between two equally delicate blades of grass.

Is there any discontent and unrest here; any hurry or frustration? Could this scene be considered a nightmare?

No; it's all part of the normal, everyday activities of the natural world.

In the main, imagining this kind of scene makes us feel relaxed, and often creates the desire to be part of it. We all experience feelings of peace every now and then, whether or not we give thought to them.

Why is it, after a much-needed holiday at the beach or in the mountains, that we take a while to readjust to our normal daily grind? Could it be because something deep inside feels at home in these natural surroundings and is reluctant to be dragged away: back into an environment that suddenly seems unreal?

Then there's the feeling we experience when stopped in our tracks by the sight of a glorious sunset or a brilliant rainbow set against a brooding sky.

Have you ever wondered about this?

We might not question such feelings when they occur, but nevertheless they leave their mark. In fact, they're probably the nearest we have come to realising there's another side to the nature of our lives. Yet, due to the ever-present pressures of our daily urban existence, we're unable to recognise their significance. So we dismiss them, and allow ourselves to be caught up in the hustle and bustle again. That is, until the next time.

You could say those country critters are to be envied.

Life on this fair planet successfully evolved long before modern man arrived on the scene. Other forms of life just get on with living, doing what has to be done, without question or doubt, at peace with their environment and free; that is, free of human intervention. It is common knowledge that the balance of nature is only upset when man interferes, so does nature really need us?

The supposedly lesser forms of life have simple minds (those with minds at all), simple needs and, environmental factors permitting, generally want for nothing. All they require for their day-to-day living becomes available as and when they have a need of it.

Some people might suggest they don't know any better, or that they can't think for themselves. But do we humans know any better, really? What have our minds done for us through the centuries? Life in the Western world may nowadays be more comfortable, allow us to travel further and faster than ever before; to broaden our knowledge or outlook on life, and definitely to enjoy better health; but as individuals we're not all that better off for it.

Humanity is not exactly more confident or secure as a result of modern technology. And we are yet to luxuriate in a greater sense of freedom than in the past.

Even technological advancement doesn't equate to greater personal wisdom. There are millions of people in the world today who've had little or no formal education and are happy enough. We certainly can't claim to be any wiser than they are.

If you *do* think Westerners are better off, ask yourself this: Why are we rarely satisfied, no matter what our situation? Why does life at times seem like a bad dream and create within us a sense of isolation? What is the reason behind our inability to accept all that life has to offer, as other living creatures do?

After all, we are a part of the natural world, starting off as a branch on the evolutionary tree when modern man deviated from the line of his predecessors.

Our earliest ancestors didn't have heart conditions, ulcers, nervous breakdowns or strokes because of the pressures of their lifestyle. They would no doubt have had accident and illness, but so do we. They weren't clock-watchers, feel they had to do something because it was the current trend, or adhere to the traditions that have been handed down from generation to generation. Their simple lives, although based on survival, were reasonably straightforward. They would not have felt the need to crave something they didn't have, or escape somewhere for a bit of peace and quiet. They just got on with what had to be done, at their own pace and guided by their instincts; without needless worry, hurry and frustration.

Today, we have so much more in our favour, and are still unable to cope with the pressures of life. Will we be better off in decades to come when technology is even more advanced? And are we really likely to feel a greater sense of freedom in the future than we do now?

Oh, that we could turn back the clock and relive those uneducated but unhurried days of early man; we might learn something from them. Why should we now be so different from our ancestors? Our anatomies are pretty much the same as theirs. Our emotions certainly haven't changed – love, fear, happiness, sorrow and anger. Where is the difference?

Could it be in our minds? Theirs were uncluttered; ours are far from uncluttered.

Admittedly, the human mind has done some wonderful things over the millennia, but it has also been responsible for our undoing; for our being trapped in the nightmare. What else could it be? In most respects we're the same as our early human counterparts. Whatever made them tick also makes us tick, yet you wouldn't think so now.

That 'part of nature' aspect of our identity seems to have been mislaid somewhere along the evolutionary line. Everything else on this planet exists without undue strife, but we don't.

Again, could it be because of our minds?

It's true we've evolved with intelligent, useful minds that are frequently put to good use. We can think for ourselves, and for others too, when necessary. We keep our minds energised with a range of activities; but too often this also means we're overloading already weary brains.

Yes, our minds are an anatomical marvel, but they can only stand so much bombardment. Could that be one of the reasons we suffer so much from stress?

What happened to that good-old standby human instinct? The achievements of early humans arose mainly from the use of their instincts and observations; working things out intuitively and evolving accordingly.

Has this been overlooked by modern humans?

And what about some of the earliest discoveries or inventions; not forgetting the major building projects of ancient times? Where did their know-how come from? Some might suggest from aliens; but certainly not from a manual.

Successive generations of human beings have devised countless written or unwritten rules for all aspects of life, and are still doing so. When do we get a chance to use our own inbred human instinct or intuition? Whatever you prefer to call this, it's inbred in every one of us.

We all know it is there; it's bursting to get out, to be recognised: to be free. But we're constantly forced to hold it back by pressures all around us; pressures from parents, teachers, employers and partners; from our children and our peers; from institutions, community, local culture, the media and, of course: advertising.

If we were able to respond to our own instincts right from the start we wouldn't experience that sense of indecision; of being trapped. We wouldn't need to lash out at all that goes against the grain, like a cornered dog that doesn't want to react badly but has no choice.

Freedom is a natural right – our right.

The deep-rooted nature of human beings is to be free and unfettered, not chained or channelled to the point where often we feel the need to cry out 'Enough!' in sheer desperation.

The apathy, resentment, arrogance, and many more of our negative behaviour patterns, often exist because of the pressures or restrictions, the absence of affection and understanding; not forgetting the traditions, trends and lifestyles that are so common in our world today. These have little to do with the thinking, feeling identity they're supposed to relate to: the person we each call 'me.'

Surely, the best way to learn anything is by experience, even if we make mistakes in the process.

What is 'learning by experience,' anyway?

It doesn't necessarily mean falling down the manhole on the footpath in order to discover it's there, but that we should be able to realise its existence for ourselves rather than being told by someone else. We need to experience the true realities of life in our own instinctive way; in other words: to be free.

Perhaps that's what real freedom is – to be given the chance to respond to our highest instincts, our own better nature; to be allowed the opportunity to wake up to the reality of our own lives.

The inner 'Self' longing to be free of outside pressures.

The birds of the air are free; likewise the fish in the sea. Even a tiny worm in the garden is free. How can a worm be free when we, its evolutionary superiors, are not?

And where does this freedom and motivation come from? It does have a specific source.

Their motivation doesn't come from some influence outside their own being, but from within them. A tree draws nutrients from the soil into its roots; then up through the trunk and branches, and out to the leaves. It uses its environment to its own advantage yet relies on no outside help to achieve this. Try watching the progress of a seed potato that's been set aside to sprout prior to planting. It sits on the shelf all by itself and sprouts. It is alive; it's growing; and 'something' is making it do this. Even a scruffy little seed potato is sustained from within itself, with not a sign of soil or water.

Are we so *very* different?

An army of ants on the move throughout a forest is completely self-sustaining, motivated and ordered in the way it operates. In some respects their structure of life is similar to ours; but they don't have an intellect to work things out. They are served only by their individual and collective instincts.

What is instinct, anyway?

It's that invisible something within nature that guides, protects and sustains, and it does a pretty good job.

Some people call it 'Mother Nature.'

It's instinct that motivates birds to flock together in autumn and fly thousands of miles to their destination without the aid of a map. It is instinct that initiates spring growth; nobody's around to push the appropriate button. And instinct brings a newborn lamb to its feet moments after birth. What we call 'instinct' has successfully evolved generation after generation of animals and plants, in fact, anything that has ever had the essence of life flowing through it, for millions of years.

Not a bad record for something we can't even see.

If every form of nature that isn't human can rely on this source of motivation, then why can't we? Humans are above all other forms of life, or so we're led to believe. If the 'something in nature' looks after the lower forms so well, then it stands to reason that it would do even more for us if given the chance.

We don't give it the chance, though. We're all too busy, muddling along by our own devices or following current trends; oblivious of what we're doing to ourselves and of what we're missing.

We seem to think that we alone (that is, our conscious minds: our egos) should make all the decisions and provide all of our answers. Yet it's also true that when asked to comment on a burning issue or how we intend to handle a tricky situation, we so often have to say, "I don't know." How then can we possibly work out the answers to all of life's most difficult questions? At times, even the simplest domestic problem weighs too heavily for us to think about, let alone resolve.

What's more, we seek instant answers, when many of the solutions to our problems really need time; plenty of time before they can effectively be achieved.

When we don't know how to solve a problem, wouldn't it be nice if we could hand it over to someone else? Yet, if only we realised it, we would see that this is *precisely* what we can do. In fact, if satisfactory solutions are to be found, this is exactly what we *should* do. We wouldn't need to consult another person or any kind of institution, but the invisible 'something,' whatever it really is, that's present in and sustains every living thing, including us.

Unfortunately our minds, so intent on going their own way, don't ease off long enough to give our instincts the opportunity to surface.

Perhaps if you or I were completely alone in the world, as though in a real fortress, we might stand a better chance of working out a few things for ourselves. We would have no alternative but to learn our lessons in life; and probably the hard way, too.

Yet, we are rarely alone. Mostly we live amongst other people: with our families, in impersonal cities and with current trends; amongst a diversity of people or situations that so often dominate our thinking.

So much is expected of us by others, to the extent that sometimes it seems like a 'Big Brother' is waiting to clamp down if we don't toe the line. Yet by the same token, don't we also expect a lot of ourselves, and become impatient when we fail to perform each time with robotic precision? Every day there are new pressures in one area of life or another: new stresses and strains coming into our minds from all directions – and going out as well.

You know how it goes: keep your weight down, be careful with your budget, watch your speed; be culturally or politically aware. And then there's conservation.

Must conform; must be concerned; must reduce the cost; must take care.

...And this we call living?

The mind of today's Westerner is like a pressure cooker, but with one tragic difference.

In a pressure cooker the steam builds up until it reaches a certain level, when the safety valve comes into operation to let out excess steam and keep the whole thing safe. Our minds differ from this in that we don't allow pressure to escape from them as we should. Instead, it keeps building up inside the mind, creating more and more stress until we feel as if it's going to explode.

Where is our safety valve? Where is that freedom of the individual: that freedom of self-expression? Why do we feel we must make these choices that so often go against the grain, merely because it's the latest trend, or because somebody somewhere says we should?

Like sheep we follow the leader because we don't know what else to do. But we're not simple-minded sheep; we're freethinking individuals, able to cultivate our own private aspirations and deepest convictions – or at least, we should be.

...So why?

Perhaps it's habit. Almost everything in our lives is just that: acquired habits piled one on top of the other; not only in our daily routines, but in our general thinking, too.

We have inherited this sheep-like attitude from our predecessors or peers to the extent that we're now unable to break free and think for ourselves. If this has become ingrained in the Western psyche, then it's no wonder we are unable to cope. It's no wonder we don't make contact with our instincts, and it's of little wonder that we now find ourselves immersed in a nightmare.

But, the miracle of it all, and the first real step towards an awakening, is the recognition that this is not of our own doing. It became embedded in us long before the day of our birth.

So at last we can breathe a sigh of relief, let go some of the stress, and begin to study the situation objectively.

RELEASE OF THE MIND

It would seem, then, that many of us are caught up in the nightmare of human conditioning, and would probably like to break free of it if given the opportunity. Unfortunately, though, positive changes cannot occur while we are still bogged down with everyday pressures.

So, if we can't do anything to change our environment or even the attitudes and opinions of others, what can we actually do about it?

Let's not beat about the bush here. We really need to start by taking a good look at *ourselves*; or rather, by reviewing what's in our poor cluttered minds. Maybe then we'll be able to get rid of some unwanted junk.

When I was in the depths of depression I could not properly evaluate anything. My mind seemed to be so thickly clouded that I suspected I'd never see clearly again. I shut off all positive thoughts, and dampened down every emotion except anger. Dominated by negatives, I became immune to any suggestion that I was merely disillusioned about my life because the negativity in my mind was too much to bear.

Once the negative feelings and introverted attitudes began to clear, everything around me, although in itself unchanged, appeared in a different light.

They say that half the cure for any ailment, be it physical or psychological, lies in the first place in knowing what's wrong; so let's start there.

You may think this would be impossible because we're all different. Yet, although our personalities, lifestyles and so on differ considerably, beneath our diverse exteriors there is an identity that's common to us all and which shares the same problems.

What is a problem anyway? In most cases it's an issue we cannot cope with or to which we can't find a solution.

Everybody has problems of one kind or another. Some are trivial, some are immense. Even though our individual actions and reactions to the problems may be different, inwardly we each experience a similar effect from them.

Through feelings of insecurity, we each strengthen our emotional fortress walls, behind which the ego hides. Occasionally we fire out at the world with harsh and unkind words, but withdraw rapidly to the safety of the battlements at the first sign of adversity. And woe-betide anyone who dares to encroach on our territory.

If we only recognised it, though, there are other people behind other fortress walls with the same problems as us. All it needs is a hint of understanding, a carefully aimed sympathetic word, a morsel of caring or a feeling of trust, to bring these walls tumbling down.

We know we share problems. Most of us at some time or other have come across someone with similar problems to their own. And isn't it great to be able to sit down and get them out into the open with someone you can relate to? You can chat with a virtual stranger and quickly discover you have something in common – an experience, an interest or maybe an outlook – that brings down your respective walls and transforms two isolated strangers into friends.

Yes, talking is a great tonic, but it isn't always possible to sit down and get things off your chest like that. Let's face it: some people wouldn't even want to.

When a problem is vague and not easily definable, it often helps to sit down with a piece of paper or at the computer and jot down whatever it is that's bothering you.

Bottling up those feelings makes the problem seem insurmountable. However, getting them out into the open by writing them down, with no-one else around, is as beneficial as shouting them from the rooftops. You don't have to be a literary genius – one word is enough to start with. Even Tolstoy must have begun his epic 'War and Peace' with a first word. Once the ice is broken and that word set down, you could find the problem pours onto the page of its own accord.

Writing is also a good means of releasing some stress, especially if it concerns a problem that is personal and that you'd have difficulty discussing with someone else. You could try writing down what's the worst thing that could happen in relation to your problem. You might discover that it's not so bad after all. You don't have to be careful what you say or how you say it. There's nobody around to criticise, to be offended or to misunderstand. Unless you want them to, nobody else will read it. What's more, you may even find that by writing it down and then reading it back again, you're able to see the solution for yourself.

When we live with a situation day in day out, whether self-inflicted or not, the automatic reaction is to want to escape: to drink, to drugs, to the side or arms of someone sympathetic and understanding, and even to the other side of the world. We can feel trapped by people or by circumstances, trying to escape from them because we're no longer able to relate to them. Or else we cling to them in desperation; suddenly feeling insecure.

Everyone longs for freedom and peace of mind; for a sense of fulfilment in ourselves, or for the great void within us to be replenished. There's little in life more important than feeling complete. To feel empty is to be trapped; to be trapped is to feel dead inside.

The inability to achieve a sense of fulfilment can drag us down to levels where we have little hope of achieving our own potential. We can become what heartless people label 'losers.' If this is so, then surely we must all be losers, because at some time or another we've all been pulled down in this way.

When it happens, our natural response is to seek out others to whom we can relate with ease, whether in a city night club, the local sports arena or a women's institute. In these sorts of places we hope to find what we seek: companionship, understanding, a feeling of belonging, or even a sense of security.

Loneliness and insecurity may drive us to affiliate with our own kind; but we also cling to abstract things, such as memories of enjoyable evenings or restful holidays. They might be chance meetings with people with whom we seemed to click, or days when we experienced a brief but rewarding sense of complete freedom. We sometimes long to or even try to relive the experience of them, because our daily lives are so lacking in one way or another that we don't get that sense of fulfilment and freedom, which is a natural right.

But all of this has its basis in our minds rather than in reality. It's the attitude that, in reacting to stress, creates the problem.

A problem shared is a problem halved, because the mind is relieved of some of the pressure. A problem coped with or resolved ceases to be a problem.

Our weary minds dominate us because, not being psychologists, we don't know how they work or how to put things right. We fail to allow for our natural human weaknesses, and then give up at the first sign of adversity because it all seems so hopeless. Yet in reality it's not hopeless, but merely the product of an unhappy mind.

Unwittingly we give power to our minds and they work against us; whereas it should be, and could be the other way round. Literally speaking, we are our own best friends or our own worst enemies.

Many years ago I hurt my back shifting furniture. Time went by with no let-up from the excruciating pain. On many occasions, when my children were still small and totally dependent on me, the pain became unbearable. I convinced myself that I needed an operation but that it was out of the question with children to look after. For six weeks I was in agony, and made myself a nervous and physical wreck. In the end I could stand it no longer and went to the doctor. He knew instantly what was wrong, prescribed anti-inflammatory painkillers and two pills later the pains subsided. For my part, I had got it all wrong. My overloaded mind had jumped to its own conclusions.

Later on, I could not believe that I had allowed my mind to dominate my rational thinking. Once the situation was viewed from a better perspective and with the right course of action taken, I made a complete recovery; which also boosted my self-esteem.

On the other hand, isn't the opposite also true? Don't we sometimes inadvertently assert control over our minds when it suits our purpose?

For instance, consider this: You've got a nasty cold. You are miserable and only want to sleep it off. Suddenly a friend calls. He's won some money on Lotto, would like to celebrate and wants you to join him. Will you ever! You'd be up, dressed and out the door before you knew it, cold forgotten.

Do you see the difference? Isn't this a form of control, even if it isn't done consciously? Drawing the attention away from the problem could be all that is needed to prevent your weary mind from sinking into an unhappy and unwanted rut.

If a child hurts itself, the parent might say, "Let's kiss it better." I remember my own mother doing this when I was little. I used to associate the getting better with the *kiss*: that miracle-wonder cure. Yet, with the benefit of adult hindsight the truth is obvious. The real cure was brought about by the fact that once the hurt was kissed better, I dismissed it from my mind. In other words, I *forgot* about it and it no longer hurt.

Matter over mind, or mind over matter; the choice is ours. We each have the capacity to take control of our thoughts if we could recognise it. Nothing and nobody else has a hold on our minds.

On national television these days we're bombarded with infomercials: those irritating and lengthy adverts. Dealing with them is simple: we can switch them off using the remote. Dealing with invasive thoughts is not as simple. We might never be able to avoid worrying situations, but our minds remain our own.

All we have to do is say "No."

Say *no* over and over again, and mean it, when the mind is in danger of jumping to wrong conclusions or giving in to its whims and fancies, and we soon begin to recognise our own potential. All that's needed, when a thought, a situation or a phobia has us in its grip, is to stand up to it and affirm: "You have no hold over me." In time, with perseverance and maybe a bit of guidance, the hold will lessen.

Intrinsically, we are ourselves. I am not just the name my parents gave me; I'm also myself: sacred and untouchable. You are also *yourself:* sacred and untouchable.

The 'I' that is me, and the 'I' that is you cannot be adversely affected unless our minds permit disturbing influences to do so.

Yet, it goes without saying that where we have specific obligations – like a parent and child situation, the law of the land, a driver on the road or workplace requirements and so on – we can't be as untouchable as we would like. The expression, 'When in Rome do as the Romans do' applies in all sorts of situations.

In spite of external influences, we do still have a choice. We can either allow our difficulties and conflicts to get us down, or we can calmly remain detached and unmoved; in control of our emotions, and even see the funny side.

It really is up to us.

It's also up to us what thoughts we choose to hold in our minds. We can take a piece of harmless information, perhaps a comment someone has made, and blow it up by constantly thinking about it. Or we can decide whenever the thought comes to mind that it's not worth getting stressed over. Then, if appropriate, we can simply forget about it.

It doesn't *sound* simple? Okay, look at this:

Imagine a cup of coffee. If you put a spoon in and begin to stir, the liquid goes round and round, developing its own momentum. Even when you've removed the spoon the liquid keeps going round, and can take a while to stop, depending on how vigorously you stirred it. Unwanted thoughts are the same. You might consciously set them aside, but they're still circulating within your head.

Have you ever woken up during the night, begun to dwell on an issue, and then found you can't get back to sleep? Cast out the unwanted thought before it develops its own momentum by visualising something abstract. Force yourself if necessary. This should leave the mind comparatively peaceful.

When you come to think of it, if every train of thought we have in a single day were to develop a momentum of its own, then no wonder at times we can't think straight.

These are simple but effective methods of controlling the mind's complicated machinery. Granted, it does take time and practice – nothing is achieved overnight – but it is possible and definitely worth the effort.

When you are buried under a mound of pressures, the idea of clawing your way out seems hopeless and not worth considering: it would be so much easier to open a bottle of something for a quick fix. But if you always seem to be at rock bottom, where else is there to go but *up*?

It's like breaking in a horse. At first it resents all efforts to control it and struggles furiously. But with perseverance on the part of the trainer, eventually it has to give in. The horse has very little choice; and neither do our thought processes. The mind is subservient to a stronger, higher will which deep down inside we all possess; and that is the intuitive will of the human Self.

Relaxation also plays its part in clearing the mind of debris. This was definitely something I learnt the hard way.

At one stage on my journey towards awaking from the nightmare, when life seemed to be driving me crazy, I sought professional help. To begin with I consulted my doctor who put me on anti-depressants. These helped, but I resented how they deadened thoughts and reflexes that were still sound. Then I heard about hypnotherapy and decided to give it a try. I went to the clinic for an hour almost daily for a fortnight. The therapist assured me that great things can be achieved under hypnosis. Well, maybe I was subconsciously stubborn or something, but she couldn't even hypnotise me. So much for her claims. Yet, still we persevered, and the experience proved to be a valuable stage in my journey for this reason:

The therapist had me sit motionless and do nothing except focus my thoughts, for a whole hour at a time; something I had never done before. At first it was torture. I felt as though I was a tightly wound up coil that wanted to spring free. But as the days went by my entire physical and mental make-up calmed down. By the end of the final appointment I was composed and peaceful, perhaps for the first time in my life. I felt a wonderful sense of release, and was by all accounts a completely different person.

Relaxation is hard to achieve when you're tensed up and not used to doing it. In fact, it's almost painful. But with perseverance it can bring about the most incredible effects on the entire body, creating a state of mind that is relaxed, receptive and ready to step onto the next rung on the ladder to freedom. However, this can only be achieved when we've voluntarily made the first move.

And it couldn't be easier than this: To acknowledge in ourselves that we desire freedom from the fortress of our minds.

After all, when opportunity knocks and something desirable is offered on a plate, we still have to make an effort to get off the couch and open the door.

We have to do something for ourselves, even if it's only making a simple but vital decision.

IT CAN HAPPEN TO YOU

When we have achieved some control over our thoughts, we can confidently claim to be well on the way towards awaking from the nightmare.

Awareness of activity within the mind will result in fewer disturbances than before, and even affords us an occasional sense of tranquillity. Once this occurs we're ready for the next stage, which is allowing our instincts to come to the surface where they belong.

At the moment they're unable to get through because of a 'blockage.' This could be compared with blood vessels clogged with cholesterol. As we begin to take care over what we put into the body, along with adequate exercise, the subsequent effect on the entire system is beneficial.

Likewise, clear the mind and our natural instincts are able to perform as intended.

Understanding some of the principles involved with the healing process, and then putting them into practice, will certainly ease the pressure, but it's only a part of it. We may also feel unsure about who we are, what we're doing here and where we're heading. This is where our instincts play a primary role.

We know we have instincts: it's the invisible force that tugs at us and conflicts with impulsive or invasive thought.

Yet, most of the time we don't listen to our instincts as we should.

They say that if you want a job done properly, do it yourself. I would add to this: when you want to get answers to your problems or to know what's best for you, then ask yourself; or more precisely, consult your *inner* Self. Talk to your inner resources: your instincts, your intuition; call it what you will. It's within all of us and in everything that exists.

Our human instinct comes from somewhere, and not from any external source. A plant instinctively draws up all it needs for survival without conscious thought; likewise a bird or animal in its natural environment. Similarly the instinctive, intuitive side of our human identity can be far more influential than we've previously given it credit for. Through our instincts we're able to glean all that we need whether in the form of confidence, health, insight; or even money. Neither does it arrive on a cushion of cloud or by means of a thunderbolt, but through ordinary, everyday channels.

Does this sound far-fetched?

Perhaps it will, if you've never thought along these lines before.

In any aspect of our lives we can only judge by what we're used to. As far as daily needs are concerned, we're used to earning money to buy clothes, food, etc., and to provide shelter or entertainment for ourselves and our families. We are therefore used to attributing our success, financial or otherwise, to our own efforts and ideas. Rarely does it occur to us that any other influence might be involved. Yet how often do we attribute our fortunes to good luck or coincidence: things turning up with no logical explanation, or just 'there' when we need them?

Are these occurrences really of our own doing?

Animals in the wild don't attribute success to their own efforts; somehow they're led to food and shelter. In the main, they are supplied directly or indirectly with all they need, even if they have to rummage for it. Human beings differ only in that we've developed a monetary system to ensure a reasonably fair share for each of us. Yet we are still directly or indirectly supplied with, or are given the opportunity to acquire, all that we need.

Opportunities for success may hammer loudly on the door or quietly form as an idea. They might start with an advertisement in a paper or can only be reached after a great deal of effort.

A need of something develops, and we begin to attract it. We draw this to us because, just as plants and animals receive without question, so do we receive it as the result of a universal law – the most natural law in existence; although we frequently seem oblivious of it in relation to ourselves.

When we take in food, the body absorbs what it needs from the food and eliminates the rest. So do we, without conscious thought, absorb whatever we need from our inner resources as and when we need it. The law only ceases to operate properly when we block off the flow by worry, irrational thinking and failure to acknowledge the law.

This is why so many of us in our Western culture are poor or sick, lonely and unhappy; because the law is not operating in our lives as it should.

Call it a life-force, an energy, a presence, or whatever word you feel comfortable using, the invisible law is the motivating factor behind everything that exists within our minds, our world and our universe. It is the *rule*.

Our actions and thoughts, both past and present, are the *exception* not the rule. The rule remains; the law is always operating. We have the choice of whether to remain the exception or once again be part of the rule.

No one person is favoured or rewarded above another, although at times we're inclined to think so. For instance, in an ocean-going yacht race involving boats of complex design and crews of experienced sailors, each sailor knows he must obey the rules of the sea. The ocean isn't going to reward him above all others for obeying its rules: he still might lose the race. If he does obey the rules, he is able to use the sea to great advantage and for a safe passage. And this also applies to his competitors.

But if the sailor doesn't bother to follow the rules and something goes wrong, he has only himself to blame. If there were rules he didn't know about and as a result he got into difficulty, the sea wouldn't let him off because of his ignorance, he'd go down like anyone else. His only choice is to follow the rules and live, or ignore them and risk drowning.

In theory what could be simpler? The hard part is putting the principles into practice; and this is something that needs perseverance and understanding.

We may talk about searching for the truth or craving freedom, but what we don't realise is that what we're seeking, whether personal liberty or the meaning of life, is around us and deep within us right now. We have merely failed to recognise it and follow its very simple rules.

Imagine you've just bought a new hi-tech gadget of some description. You don't know how it works, but are keen to try it out. You fiddle with it, and do what you think should be done to set it in motion. Yet all you achieve is frustration and the knowledge that you've gummed up the works. Then you find the instructions sheet. You sit down with gadget and instructions, and start to read. Eventually you discover your mistakes, gain an understanding of how the thing works, and begin to use it properly.

So it is with us. The instructions for living were with us all along, yet we haven't bothered to refer to them. As a result we don't understand how the rules of life work and how to relate them to our own lives. This is not a new concept, it has existed since the world began; merely needing now to be revisited and more fully understood.

It's not that people don't believe there is some kind of order to life, but rather we can't relate to something that's invisible and without apparent substance. So we look for our answers in things that are visible, tangible and easy to understand.

The human mind, though a product of evolutionary magic, can grasp only a limited amount. Can you envisage the size of the universe, of our fair planet or even the size of the pyramids? On their own, such dimensions cannot be grasped. They need to be compared with something of a familiar size; for example, if you photographed someone standing on a pyramid. Similarly, we need to compare the infinite invisible with something.

We're used to dealing with the tangible, so we try to find a comparison in the tangible. But the infinite invisible cannot be compared. It's a separate dimension. Except for the wonders of nature there is nothing visible to compare it with.

We look to things that can easily be put into words, but these, too, defy description. They require comprehension that doesn't come naturally to an overworked mind.

Consider the law of gravity, which is now very much taken for granted. In olden times this was a concept beyond the grasp of ordinary folks, but once understanding became common knowledge, there also developed a respect for its rules.

If we could begin to accept this natural law as readily as we now accept the law of gravity; if we could follow the rules and give this unseen, intangible energy the chance to re-enter our lives, for it is still there albeit veiled from our conscious minds, then the sense of imprisonment would gradually dissolve and in time cease to exist.

We would begin to awaken to life as it really is, and not how we've perceived it to be in the nightmare.

It's the influence of the material world and everything we now accept that keeps us imprisoned or prevents us from awakening.

If we were to open up the invisible channel between the thinking mind and our inner resources; if we allowed truth and reality to flow *out* from us instead of taking *in* all of that superfluous information, the fortress walls would tumble, the nightmare would end, and freedom would at last be ours.

We might still live in a war-torn country or suffer under bureaucracy, but it won't adversely affect us to the same extent or drive us toward desperate measures. We would rise above the negative; our experiences no longer the problems they once seemed to be. They might still exist, but as situations to be dealt with, not wrestled with. We are able to cope, and are therefore much better off, in the same situations that once caused us stress.

Life begins to flow through the mind as freely as a stream runs over pebbles. No longer is there the need to drown our sorrows, take those pills, escape everyday drudgery, look for something better on the other side of the world, or even book a holiday. Life itself could begin to seem like a holiday.

This may sound incredible, even laughable; but it's true.

You may be thinking, "No, not me; nothing like that ever happens for me." Indeed, it would be a natural reaction. I thought along those lines for a very long time. But I was proved wrong, and finally realised it's only the inhibitions of the mind that make us think that way.

Anyway, why *shouldn't* it happen to you? Aren't we all made of the same stuff?

All seeds, when pushed into the soil, contain in their DNA everything they will need from germination to maturity and beyond. There are no exceptions. Their life doesn't come from the ground or the air: that merely provides their 'daily bread.' Remember the seed potato? It didn't even need soil.

It's the same with human babies. No enticement will make a baby walk, talk or cut its teeth before it's ready to. Only the 'something' inside knows when that time is.

With the right nurturing all a baby will need from birth onwards is embodied in its genes. This process continues intuitively throughout its lifetime without conscious effort.

Basic human instinct is part of us from the moment we're conceived, and throughout our lives. It is ever present within the mind, body and soul: sometimes active, often dormant; whether or not we're aware of it. Any thoughts or feelings that creep in to persuade us otherwise are merely tricks of the mind that lead us astray.

The truth about ourselves is within us; waiting to be released into our awareness. And the only activity that will bring this about is the 'awakening' from the nightmare.

Can you now see how the mind plays its tricks; reacting to conditions and emotions? But don't listen to your mind: it's trying to mislead you. Don't let it get the better of you; you have the capacity to rise above it.

You'll need to do it yourself, though; no-one else can do it for you. With help from the powers-that-be deep inside, you will succeed. With you at all times is your best friend in the world: your inner Self.

We've been told, 'you are what you think,' and humankind certainly appears to have adopted the concept that mind and identity are one and the same thing.

Yet this is not so. If you develop a niggling headache that you can't get away from no matter how hard you try, the pain dominates you. For a while there seems to be nothing in your life *but* the pain, and you become oblivious of all else.

...But still, the pain is *not* you.

A persistent problem is the same. It's in the mind, and it hurts – not so much in a physical way, but mentally and emotionally. It consumes you and gives the impression of being the whole you. Yet, just as physical pain is not the whole person but only a temporary state, so too is an emotional problem.

Even your mind is not you, but merely a part of you. The identity and personality that is the intrinsic 'you' is separate from the piece of equipment we call our minds.

When you are sound asleep or under anaesthetic the conscious mind is inoperative. But although your mind is switched off, the whole person certainly is not. The body continues to function normally without your help; which means it's not reliant on conscious activity for its survival. Both body and mind have their own support system deep within. And this has nothing to do with the thoughts going through your head.

In a newborn baby the conscious mind is like an empty vessel. Only instinctive impulses are present. As the infant matures, his mind is receptive to what he encounters around him and what he realises for himself. If he were to absorb this information and nothing else he would be receptive to the laws of life, and his intuition would guide him for the rest of his days.

However, the intensity of outside influences is far too strong for the discerning effects of intuition. While he's growing up his instincts become suppressed, to the extent that he later begins to question whether he possesses anything of himself at all.

Really, it's no wonder we sometimes feel we're fighting for survival; we are. And not for the survival of our bodies; we are struggling to save our real identities.

Yet, despite everything else, our instincts are still there: dormant maybe, but certainly not dead. At times they niggle away, leaving us frustrated. We can't understand what's going on, and don't know what to do about it.

We have no inkling that our inner feelings are the true guide, and all else is but part of our worldly baggage. Once we've recognised what *is* going on, decisions can be made from deep within our own being.

All we have to do is open up our minds, tune in and allow it to surface.

As human beings we set ourselves materialistic goals that we follow relentlessly, assuming we're doing the right thing. In our misguided determination we keep reaching out for whatever it is we seek, and are usually quite happy while we're aspiring to it. But if and when we eventually reach our goal, we're then confronted with the question, "Where to now? What does life hold for me now?" Too often there is no satisfactory answer.

At that point we may become frustrated. Success has left us feeling that something is missing. We could even feel guilty for being dissatisfied with all that we have; for not knowing why we feel this way or what to do about it. Our natural instincts have again been suppressed beneath the external driving force in our lives, and are therefore unable to supply any answers. So we begin to sink, losing the incentive to look for something different; then find ourselves in a rut of perplexity from which there seems to be no way out.

On the other hand, many of us start off in life with few possessions or achievements, and remain quite happy. But the mesmerism of our modern world is so strong that it eventually convinces us the materialistic lifestyle is right and that our simple approach to life must be lacking. And the end result is the same: a rut of perplexity from which we can find no way out.

So, if up until now you've been stuck in that rut, take heart. Remember: when you are down the only place to go is up, and up you will go. The dejection you're feeling is temporary and of no real substance. It could be that you are about to re-awaken into the full light of day; to be 'born again' in the fullest sense of the words; the empty vessel of your soul at last replenished.

All you need to do right now is rest assured you're a real 'somebody.' You must be; you're human. Deny that if you can. Humans are the highest of the life-forms, so obviously there must be something a bit special about you. Without question or doubt, there is real purpose to your life whether you regard yourself as a sinner or a saint, or something in-between. Life itself is embodied in you. It always has been and it always will be.

Your inner Self is your fully-charged battery: your internal energy source. So give it a chance to prove its worth:

To come to your rescue in times of need and guide you when you're undecided; to bring you peace when all around there is turmoil; to help you find your niche in life.

So get ready to enable it.

It's your inheritance, it's your right – and it's free.

OPENING OUT A WAY

When we've been entrapped in the mind's fortress or have searched outwardly for some solutions, the prospect of a different way of thinking takes some getting used to.

Just about everything in every form we nowadays take for granted was once regarded with fear and scepticism, because it was new or just different from what the people of the day were used to. Even now, when we're faced with something different we're inclined to be suspicious if it's not proven. Yet, just as humanity learnt to accept the law of gravity and other innovations, when we do become accustomed to something new and accept it into our daily lives, we can discover a whole new world.

There's even more reluctance to trust in something *abstract*. We look to the physical and the tangible for our dependencies, whether a person, an institution or even a sports team.

Rarely do we accept a principle straight away.

As we're so slow in adjusting to new ideas, the notion of turning inwards to look for help instead of searching elsewhere will need time for adjustment. Our lives are made up of habit and routine, and planning a routine for contemplation, for 'spiritual' thinking, is merely one more habit to add to the list.

Getting into or out of *any* habit requires a certain amount of self-sacrifice and effort; but not here. All that's needed in this case is a moment of time at regular intervals, plenty of patience, and a desire to be freed from the shackles that have restrained us for so long.

It takes time, practice and perseverance to reach a state of inner peace, but all natural processes take time. A deep flesh wound takes a long time to heal. On the surface it looks as though it's not getting any better, but the healing process develops from the inside outwards. Eventually the scab falls away to reveal new tissue, without any effort on our part at all.

So it is with the 'inner' healing. It won't immediately be noticeable. What's inside is well buried, and our negative influences may be reluctant to let it go. I realised that first hand when trying to unwind my nerves at the clinic.

So, don't be in a hurry. Take things one day at a time, just like the slow and steady approach recommended for weight loss. Learn to inwardly walk before you think about running. You've got your whole life in which to achieve it. But you will definitely get there if you really want to, and are prepared to stick at it.

Peace of mind, together with the sense of freedom that comes with it, is the best life experience that can happen to anyone, and it's within the grasp of everybody who is prepared to give it a try.

To make contact with the long-lost real identity, the Self that's beneath all the worry and tension; to be in touch with what makes us all tick, this truly is the 'Secret of Life.' We don't have to wait for it to come to us for it's already there. All we have to do is unlock the door to our inner being and allow it to gradually seep out into the conscious mind.

To bring this about, you first need to turn your attention inwards: gently, gradually and with only as much time and effort that you're able to give on each occasion. There are no specific techniques; each would approach it differently.

As you proceed, become aware of what feels right for you, and of anything that doesn't. There is never any need to think it's not working or that you might be wasting your time.

Our powers of concentration and frame of mind differ daily from person to person. Each of us is only capable of as much concentration as our state of mind permits. If you find you can't fit it in, there are too many distractions or you're too tired, don't worry: there's always another time, as long as you commit to that other time.

As frequently as you can manage, allow a couple of minutes, a few times a day, in order to relax and become acquainted with your inner Self. The best times are first thing in the morning when the pressures of your day have not yet built up, and last thing at night when they are over. Depending on daily routine, if you're able to you could fit in other times; whenever you're alone with your thoughts.

It's not necessary to go anywhere special, although at first it helps to isolate yourself so you can concentrate. To be honest, when everything around me is clamouring for attention, I sometimes retreat to the garden shed in order to contemplate.

The idea is to eliminate outside sounds and distractions as much as possible. You could even insert a pair of earplugs, if you want to.

Make yourself comfortable, whether you are sitting or lying down, and be sure you're warm enough. If you aren't comfortable you will find it hard to concentrate.

Now close your eyes, while remaining alert. Gradually let yourself go limp from the tip of your toes to the top of your head. If you have difficulty relaxing, breathe slowly and rhythmically, so that in time you're able to keep it up automatically without thinking about it.

This technique helps to dispel any nervous tension, and takes the mind off bodily comfort.

When the tension begins to lessen, imagine that you're basking in warm sunshine, perfectly at ease. If you can, try to stop yourself from consciously thinking. This could be difficult at first, but it's the hardest part of the exercise, and is just a question of practice. Remember the stirred cup of coffee? It's amazing how responsive your mind can be once it knows you mean business. If you're prepared to persevere and are not easily discouraged, you will soon notice the difference. Just the thought of all that you're trying to accomplish should be enough encouragement to keep going.

You don't need to stop the involuntary thoughts from circulating in your mind. This would be too hard to control, especially in the early stages. It's normal to be bothered by them, so you shouldn't be tempted to give up on account of it.

As time goes by, this mind-rambling will slowly lessen of its own accord.

...The wild horse is gradually being tamed.

The next step is to concentrate your attention, as though withdrawing into a clam shell and closing it in front of you. You could even put your hands over your face; it may help, and nobody is going to see you. If you still find it hard to concentrate, bring an object into your mind's eye. You don't need to visualise, stare or squint. You are focusing your attention, not your eyesight. Alternatively, sit in front of a window and gaze at a distant tree or some other landmark.

As soon as your concentration falters, whip it back to the object. This helps to prevent more unwanted thoughts from entering the mind. It's easier to prevent them from entering than to kick them out once firmly established.

After a few attempts you'll find you don't lose focus so readily. Your mind is beginning to respond.

Even a moment of mental relaxation is more beneficial than a shot of whisky.

Be aware that there is a force or presence within you. After all, you wouldn't even be alive now if there wasn't. Tell yourself that at this precise moment there is nothing, but nothing exterior to your shell.

Imagine the presence within you as another person. Try talking to that person sincerely and honestly as you might to a friend. Feel as much at ease as you would relaxing over a beer with your friend. You have nothing to feel awkward about, so talk and think freely. You might say something like, "Well, here I am, then. I feel a bit stupid just sitting here like this, talking to myself. I'm not sure what I'm supposed to do, but I believe that somehow you can sort out the mess I seem to be in. So now it's over to you."

It doesn't really matter what you say; even if to begin with you have to admit you don't know *what* to say. If words don't come at all, it still doesn't matter. Just remain quiet, alert and concentrating, as though listening in the stillness, for as long as you feel comfortable and at ease. Be assured that the power of life is surging through you, and your actions are helping to bring awareness of it to the surface.

In time you'll find that there are things you want to mention and questions you probably need to ask. Perhaps something of a more personal nature will come to mind, or difficulties with a relationship. Your mind may begin to dwell on an aspect of nature: how it came to be, or how life courses through it. The possibilities are endless, and all of this helps to establish the habit of turning inwards and getting the mind used to thinking along these new lines. Often the first few words stimulate thought, and others follow easily.

As soon as you find yourself fidgeting, open your eyes. Take a moment to adjust; then carry on with what you were doing beforehand. I could never relax or concentrate for more than a couple of minutes. But it's not how long that counts; it's how much we want this influence in our lives that dictates whether or not we're likely to succeed.

It isn't absolutely necessary to say or think *anything*. A bird, a worm and that humble seed potato don't have to think about what they need. The life-force within us is aware that we are turning to it, and it responds in its own way and in its own time, which is not necessarily when we think it should.

Once we're in the habit of daily contemplation, the best thing we can do for ourselves is to refrain from seeking results; and probably hardest of all: to be patient.

Nothing is going to happen in a hurry, so it's futile to anticipate an immediate improvement. We humans are impatient creatures who like everything to happen 'now if not sooner;' but time itself is relative. On its own even a minute can seem like an eternity. Yet a minute out of an hour is nothing; a day out of a year: the blink of an eye. So although progress may seem painfully slow, it's just our over-eagerness to have things happen quickly.

The words we use merely aid concentration and stimulate inner activity. Our intuition knows our needs and motives, and that's what brings results. It determines when the time is right for questions to be answered, and its power of understanding is far greater than ours will ever be. We need never worry that we aren't getting through.

Like making or breaking any habit it's hard to persevere at first, especially when we don't appear to be making any progress. But this is a continuous process, even if we're not consciously aware of it.

Gradually we become familiar with intuitive thoughts and feelings. At first it can be hard to tell if the source of activity is the ego or our intuition. Yet, this too is part of the learning curve and forward moving.

Eventually we come to recognise without doubt when our intuition has taken over, and we're therefore able to respond.

As time goes by and you're in a position to look back over a few weeks or months, you will see that there is now a slight difference in the way you feel about life and about yourself. It may be ever so slight, but it will be positive; and from then on your life will never be the same again.

A CORNER TURNED

It's when the conscious mind relinquishes the struggle and finds peace if only for brief moments, when the ego gives up trying to dominate and all is quiet, that the channels are flung open.

The awakening spirit reveals itself in subtle, natural ways. You might notice a slight improvement in health, a less pessimistic outlook on life, an awareness of not being quite so alone, or even a sense of uplift deep within you.

Your spirit may awaken with realisations about yourself, those around you and life in general; things you might not have thought about before. And when it happens, it may come as a shock to recognise that somehow you've known it all along.

You will find yourself more tolerant of other people or observing an aspect of nature. You might be less erratic in your approach to normal daily life; even cheerful for no particular reason; hence the old expression, 'being in good spirits.'

Over time we each let go of the hurry or frustration of modern living, and adopt more of a laidback approach to daily routine. It's as though a weight is being lifted off the mind. We don't tire so easily, and that 'can't be bothered' feeling occurs less often. Our daily work is no longer such a daily grind. We even start to enjoy everyday life.

When emotionally snowed under we're not able to cope with our problems, but as time goes by and this begins to ease, our inner strength builds and we are better able to cope with them. We become more resilient to hurt and emotional upset, and find ourselves riding the storm where previously we might have foundered.

Gradually, we emerge from the mind's fortress.

In doing so we may become aware of other people, too, and recognise that there's more to them than meets the eye. We are able to see through the external. This helps us to better understand how others can be just the same as us, whatever their age-group, appearance or background, and can even have the same sort of problems.

More importantly, we better understand ourselves and the workings of our own minds.

When the spirit awakens, we begin to notice activity in both factions of our minds: the unhappy, worldly ego that is trying to draw us back into previous habits, and the new higher Self that's in the process of emerging. Sometimes there seems to be a tug-of-war going on between them over which we have little control. Occasionally this causes some turmoil as we work through it; to the extent that we may wonder what on earth is going on. One minute we're on top of the world, the next minute hurled into a chasm.

The worldly self is like bad bacteria in the body that's eaten away by our own defence system. The true Self fights back and, without effort on our part, slowly releases us from the torment. So, although at the time it may seem like the end of the world, any upset we experience in the process of this renewal is in fact a new beginning. The important thing, though possibly the hardest of all, is to keep going and not dwell on obstacles that crop up.

After all, if you were ill, and the doctor said you'd need to be patient during your recovery, you would be able to accept this. During that period there'd be times when your patience is stretched thin. Yet you'd also have days of comparative calm; remaining content to let nature take its course.

This is how it goes for our inner healing: some good days and others not so good; except it's not the doctor who is telling us we need time to recover, but ourselves. The secret is not to feel discouraged, for healing *will* come in time.

You know, we think we suffer. In the main, we experience anguish or sorrow and call it 'suffering.' Often we even reel under it. But in this case, suffering is impermanent: a means to an end. It's as though one side of our personality has to be cruel to the other side in order, ultimately, to be kind. When you're well and happy it's easy to accept this state of affairs. The hard part is being objective about it when you're actually 'suffering.'

Imagine you need a filling and have reluctantly made an appointment with a dental technician. You know it will be unpleasant, but still you go because you also know it will soon be over, and then you'll experience a welcome sense of relief.

Ridding ourselves of emotional and mind pressures is like a learning curve. We find things out by experiencing them and are so much wiser. It's all very well to state, "Next week I'm going to give up chocolate," but such a statement is usually ineffective in the long run. Saying you'll do something is always much easier than actually doing it. You will have to try and fail over and over again; finally reaching a stage where you're so fed up with failure that you somehow turn a corner and set off up the road to success.

We cannot flick a switch and be instantly freed from established habits. Something needs to be transformed on the inside before we can develop lasting strength and immunity. We must experience frustration in order to get habits out of our system and allow peace to take their place. We have to resist with every fibre of our being and finally win through in order to be strong; except it's not other people we're fighting, but our own worldly nature.

Imagine you had a bucket with a thick layer of mud on the bottom. To clean it you would need to hose it out. In doing so you'd stir up the mud, and for a minute or two the problem would appear worse than it is. But gradually, as fresh water replaced muddy water, the bucket would come clean. Our deepest habits must be flushed out before the mind is left fresh and clear.

And this we call 'suffering.'

If only we had the courage to pass beyond emotional suffering to what lies ahead, we would find it much easier to deal with. We encounter problems day after day, but the difference now is that with our inner resources in control, the problems gradually ease, whereas beforehand they would have lingered indefinitely.

It's a natural, human reaction to try and avoid pain or frustration. We do everything in our power to suppress it, take our minds off it, sedate it and drown it. Far better for us is to face up to it, and allow it to take the natural course in its own way and in its own time.

Our old cat Sammy often came home injured because he'd been in a scrap with his archrival over the fence. He was obviously hurting, but he didn't moan and groan as people would. He just went away quietly, found himself somewhere to lick his wounds, and sat it out until he knew he was well enough to get back into the fray. He seemed to accept that he was hurt and that there was nothing he could do but wait for it to heal. All we humans succeed in doing by lamenting our problems is to make ourselves miserable – and also those who have to put up with us.

Naturally, not all physical and psychological ailments are as simple to overcome and would require specialised treatment. However, with the right nurturing most of us in our Western culture could probably rise above the misery in which we're inclined to wallow when we think we're suffering.

The conscious mind, its thoughts and hang-ups, establishes the day to day pattern of our behaviour. Our attitudes and state of health, whether we understand the reasons for them or not, vary so much that we can never tell from one day to the next what moods we're likely to encounter. But our moods don't really matter. They are just fleeting and superficial; the power within unmoved by them. Only the ego is upset or adversely affected.

Moods are like waves and currents in an ocean: one minute up on a crest, the next down in a trough. But the waves aren't the ocean, and neither are the currents. The ocean itself remains constant and unmoved, evolving at its own pace. This could be compared with being a spectator at a boxing match, where you're watching the two contestants do battle rather than taking part in it yourself. By maintaining a sense of detachment from your moods you're less likely to become bogged down by them. You're able to stand aside and observe your emotions rather than suffer them. And in doing so, you develop a certain amount of understanding as to their cause.

A friend once told me, "Nothing sobers you up faster than an accident." This related to an actual drink-driving incident, but it's true that when faced with some kind of crisis, we are surprisingly able to cope. Wartime heroes, decorated on returning home, often say they performed courageous acts almost without realising it. The Self calmly detaches itself from our human weakness and keeps the situation in perspective.

Instinct takes over when our human weakness, whether physical, mental or emotional, is unable to cope.

As time moves on, so do our emotional conflicts. Gradually our better nature gains the upper hand. Each recurring low day doesn't seem as low as before – and certainly not as bad as they used to be, as we become better equipped to cope.

It's like trying to climb up a sand dune. You take two steps forward and slide one back; climbing and slipping over and over, but nevertheless slowly inching ahead. If you don't give up you will eventually reach the top. When that time comes, the struggle you had in the process will seem insignificant, and you can then look out on your life with a greater panorama of understanding than you ever believed possible.

SOME PROBLEMS OVERCOME

The best way to overcome problems is to allow intuition to enlighten you, rather than work on the solution with your mind or emotions.

Imagine you were doing some gardening and came across a deep-rooted dandelion that you wanted to get rid of. If you grasped just the top of the plant you would finish up with a handful of leaves, and in time it will grow again. To remove the whole thing, you should ignore the leaves and aim straight for the root, gently persuade it to let go its hold; then root, leaves and all would come away cleanly.

The same applies with our problems. To deal with the symptoms of disease, give up the drugs or take up a hobby in order to escape them, is like pulling the dandelion by its leaves. To go to the root of the problem and remove that is to allow ourselves to be lifted up from within. When this has been accomplished the symptoms are much easier to deal with. This sounds simple, perhaps *too* simple. In fact, the degree of the lifting up depends on the degree of reliance on this source. But even the slightest lift can bring on a positive effect; something that can't be achieved so well by conventional treatment alone.

Up until now we've probably been fighting a losing battle, trying and failing in too many areas; perhaps even setting ourselves standards of achievement that are way beyond our current capabilities. Added to this are the overwhelming odds we're regularly faced with but can't control. Yet, we shouldn't try to force changes, but merely be aware of them and earnestly seek relief, in the sure knowledge that an invisible force is at work.

Once the need of help is quickened, the root of the problem begins to come away.

The ability to prevent tension and pressures building up; to remain detached and therefore be freed from them is a wonderful achievement. But as and when such pressures do infiltrate, we should neither suppress nor fight them.

As a saying goes, 'if you suppress something, you don't bury it dead – you bury it alive.'

First of all there should be a feeling of stillness and peace, even just for a moment. We need to reach a stage where we can discern and respond to our own intuition, thereby drawing the solution from deep within. And the only obstacle in the way of achieving this is that tiresome mind.

No experience in everyday life would remain untouched by this new awareness. The issues for which we reap the benefits are so varied that an attempt to list them would be futile. However, outlined in the following sections are some of the concerns that we often encounter. Individual experience will differ, but how to begin finding a solution is always the same:

COMMUNICATION

These days communication between people can be a real problem. Too often we strive to get the better *of* our fellow human beings, instead of trying to get on better *with* them. As individuals we withdraw into our fortresses to such an extent that we've got out of the habit of talking with each other on a friendly basis. We become so isolated that when a difficulty arises we have nobody to discuss it with, except perhaps on Twitter. Feelings quickly become suppressed or bottled up, and can't escape the pressure-cooker of the mind. Instead of keeping thoughts and feelings out in the fresh air of life we allow them to build up.

The problems are there, the feelings are there, but not the understanding.

Surely nobody chooses to remain isolated or miserable? Wouldn't we *all* prefer to communicate well with the inhabitants of other fortresses? Yet, the reason we fail to communicate properly may not be because we don't want to, but because we don't know how to.

Even if we're able to put our feelings into words, there is still the problem of saying what we mean in such a way that our listener can understand. How often, when talking to someone, do we lose the thread of what we're saying? In an unguarded moment it's easy to exaggerate or to be critical, thereby causing a negative reaction in the listener, because our comments have been taken literally.

And aren't we equally capable of taking others too literally? We might home in on a comment that displeases us without clarifying what the other person means, and without allowing for another's awkwardness when trying to make conversation.

Yes, we're all susceptible to a slip-of-the-tongue.

We might know what we want to say, but somehow it doesn't come out right. A hasty remark is made, and then it's too late to take the comment back. What's more, if it doesn't come out right, do we graciously apologise for the slip and accept our failings? More likely, we will either feel inadequate or become defensive. And when our listener gets the wrong end of the stick, do they tell you? No; off they go and complain about you to all their friends. Then the next time you meet one of them, you are greeted with a rebuff instead of a friendly wave.

"What did I do?" you may ask. "Was it something that I said?"

Or are you more likely to grumble, "What on earth's got into *her*?"

If we give ourselves a moment to collect our thoughts; to allow intuition to channel the words we mean and then speak them out confidently, what we're trying to say is more likely to be understood. And when we are the listener, if we relax and allow what's being said to gently flow through our minds, we don't home in on those comments or miss out on hidden truths. We're less likely to be upset by trivialities. Then, if by chance something offensive is implied, we'll react more rationally.

Many a friendship and marriage have come to grief due to hasty reactions in an argument.

With time, it's possible to remain calm, no matter what form the onslaught on your senses takes. That's a kind of freedom in itself: to 'keep your head when others are losing theirs.'

Getting on with other people

This links back to communication. The difficulties that arise stem from a lack of understanding of each other: of how we tick, our motives, our desires and our standards. It's human nature to see more faults than graces in our fellow man. We easily become blind to the finer points in family and friends, and often use comments that displease us as weapons against them; ultimately destroying what could have been good and meaningful relationships.

Not only individuals live in fortresses. Whole families can become cloistered in them, too; and each group of family members would have its own way of living. Certain types of family may appear similar on the surface, whilst the intricacies of their lives differ.

Often we cannot understand how the lives of other families could be so different from our own, and yet still be acceptable. Instead we judge them according to our own standards and way of life. If something belonging to another's lifestyle doesn't match our own, we can feel quite inhospitable towards the people concerned.

How we are to others and how they react to us can affect our day to day living. A difference of opinion with a colleague at work might generate a 'heavy' atmosphere throughout the office. Unpleasant gossip about a nearby neighbour may cause apprehension and suspicion. Being aware you've 'put your foot in it' with your teenager will definitely set the scene for days to come. All of this is brought about by unintended narrow-mindedness towards each other.

It's so easy to see only our own point of view, and not be open to the fact that other people's may differ – and that they're entitled to both hold and voice such different opinions.

Sometimes we feel a need to make friends with those around us, even forcing our attention on them in an effort to gain their respect. Yet this rarely works. If anything, it's likely to have an opposite effect. We might even drive them away with insistent or obsessive behaviour.

We can alienate others when we try to alter them to our specifications. Parents frequently do this with their children. How many fathers are resentful when sons don't want to take over the family business? Controlling wives or girlfriends have been known to try and manipulate their partners, too.

Mistakenly we assume that family and friends will meet our expectations, as though it's their duty to do so; a debt to be repaid, even.

"Is this all the gratitude you show me after everything I've done for you?"

A common exclamation in any household.

Receiving from other people, whether it's in the form of support, charity, love or respect, cannot be achieved by forceful behaviour, but rather by helpfulness, loving and letting go. By considering, understanding and accepting not what we all should be, or may be, or could be; but what we are.

The more we ask of others, the less likely we are to receive from them. The less we expect, the greater the probability that one day they will freely give.

When we seek a high standard of behaviour from other people and they let us down, we are disappointed. But if we expect little and are let down, the disappointment is minimal.

So, if we free others from our expectations, we gain a sense of freedom, too.

People tend to be creatures of moods, standards and habits; some deep-rooted and hard to shift. When we hold on to such trying habits, we reduce our chances of living peaceably with others. Yet, although we need help with this, very often the people who are in the best position to help are the ones we're least likely to listen to.

Our attitudes and opinions, sometimes deep-rooted; often ever changing, aren't to be found under the headings of medicine, psychology or even therapy. They go much deeper than that. They result from our unconscious desire to awaken from the nightmare, but show up as fortress defences. So it isn't outside help and advice that will bring about the results we seek. It's a change of outlook, and the inspiration that comes with it. With time that could mean a complete reversal of our general attitude towards life itself – and this is essentially an 'inner' thing.

Only by awakening to the true meaning of life will our fortresses be weakened.

Once we have discovered this hidden depth to ourselves, there's no longer any need to depend on others as we do presently. We will no longer try to influence and shape them, or hold on to the opinion that the world owes us a favour.

We'll look more to ourselves for answers. Joy will replace frustration and optimism replace despair. Our lives will seem 'half full' instead of 'half empty.' We'll listen as well as talk; sympathise rather than condemn; give instead of take. We might even find ourselves at peace with our neighbour.

And in tearing down the fortress walls, we'll open up a way for all the love, respect and companionship in the world to come flooding back in.

CONTROLLING THOUGHT PROCESSES

Has anybody ever said to you, "Why don't you think what you're doing?" Or maybe, "If you'd thought to get petrol on the way home, you wouldn't have run out."

And no doubt it has occurred to you at one time or another, "Now, why didn't *I* think of that?"

It's easy to accuse ourselves and others of not thinking, as though we should be able to call up thoughts whenever the need arises. But you can only remember to fill the petrol tank if something jogs your memory beforehand. You can only know how somebody feels when you become aware of it. You can only realise just about anything if it is first brought to your attention.

We need to be made aware of our thoughts, feelings and actions before we can begin to act on them.

A student once told me that at school she would throw down a toffee wrapper without thought, and it wasn't until she was given the job of sweeping out her classroom that she became aware of what she'd been doing. Some might say she should have known better; she should have thought about what she was doing from the start. Maybe she should; but the fact is, she didn't, and not through wilful negligence. The thought of it just didn't enter her head until she consciously realised it for herself.

What is negligence, anyway?

One definition is, 'Lack of attention and care.' That sounds deliberate – but is it?

...No doubt it is, sometimes.

Generally speaking, though, aren't we usually negligent because the thought to do or say something is not in our minds at the time we should be 'doing' or 'saying' it? Often we think of it afterwards, when it's too late. We might learn from our mistakes and remember them always. But on that first and sometimes crucial occasion our minds refuse to come up with the goods. Then we're left dangling somewhere between demonstrating wisdom beyond our years and looking foolish. This adds to feelings of exasperation or inadequacy, and the knowledge that we've let ourselves down.

There's no reason to feel like this, though. We can't *make* a thought enter our minds; it has to consciously arrive there. When it's there, we can decide whether to act on it or ignore it; but until it's safely lodged in our thinking processes, we can't do a thing.

If nobody's around to switch the thought on, then we must rely on another source of help, which is the inner source. This is even better than relying on other people, because it is limitless and already aware of everything we need to think about. All we have to do is keep open those channels between our intuition and our thinking minds, so that the inspiration behind any thought can be released and take hold. If we allow this to happen, we'll be more likely to remember the tank needs filling *before* we get to the petrol station.

Some lucky people can remember things easily; others feel inadequate because they can't. By relying on what lies within ourselves, we can expand on such limitations and so become increasingly confident in our approach to our everyday roles.

ATTAINING PEACE OF MIND

This would have to be one of the most important factors in our personal lives.

We're told, 'it's all in the mind,' and this has never been so true. Considering the stresses we each have to put up with, attaining peace of mind is an absolute must for satisfactory living.

The necessity for good mental health is afforded much credence these days. No longer is it brushed underneath the carpet, locked up in an asylum or suppressed with drugs. It is treated with the utmost sensitivity because it has finally sunk in that, to one extent or another, the stresses of life affect us all.

The ideal aim would be to prevent stresses from building up: to be in control, unemotional and even perfectly at ease in any situation. That, to me, is perfect freedom.

Just imagine it: The children are squabbling for the umpteenth time today and it doesn't frustrate you. The in-laws make a surprise visit, totally inconvenient, and you welcome them without flinching. You drop your shopping bag in a busy street and bend to gather up the scattered contents without fluster.

Unfortunately, though, many aspects of everyday life *don't* match our aspirations. As there is usually nothing we can do about it, wouldn't the perfect alternative be to feel at ease with our existing circumstances, and to be satisfied with what we've got? Wouldn't it be better if, instead of wanting things to be different, we were happy just doing everything we need to do, annoyances and all?

Nearly every situation has its potential for stress. It's deciding whether or not to keep stirring the cup of coffee that dictates how serenely we cope. Once we have recognised the problem, we can withdraw to our inner core of peace and harmony. There, we have the option of 'switching off' from haphazard thoughts, or withdrawing from the cause of stress and observing it with detachment.

We have to want it, though. We have to be prepared to say, "Okay, I've had enough. I'm not going to be brow-beaten by this anymore;" then focus on withdrawing into the sanctuary of our souls.

However, it does help to know that we will not be withdrawing to emptiness or to the loneliness of the mind's fortress; for there is nothing lonely or empty about our inner sanctuary. It's the most meaningful source of peace and reality that anyone could wish for.

THE EFFECTS OF NEGATIVE THOUGHT

In these troubling times when there seems to be so much negativity in our lives, it's easy to assume that there *is* nothing else going on. Turn on the TV, open a newspaper or log on to the Internet, and you'll be bombarded with negative incidents and how people react to them.

But this isn't the real truth about life: that is, Truth with a capital 'T.' The facts that are given to us may be true as far as world and local affairs are concerned, but that's not all there is to it. Truth in the absolute sense of the word comes from intuition and realisation. It's an invisible thing, an inner thing: a positive thing.

With the misguided belief that truth is not positive, we each build up our fortress to avoid getting hurt. Yet, in doing so we have also prevented the truth within us from revealing itself – and from seeping out to other people. We all need to both give and receive the positive side of our human nature, but the people closest to us often experience only the negative – and we of them – because the positive side is rarely visible.

At times people seem to have a 'sour' look on their faces. This doesn't necessarily mean they don't care, but that they may feel isolated by their own negativity. They might only be able to see their own problems, and either don't have time for or cannot cope with other people's problems as well as their own.

When I was still in the depths of the nightmare I had a friend whose situation in many ways was worse than mine. She received the help, sympathy and understanding of everyone around her, except me.

On the surface my life must have looked reasonably contented, because my family was comfortably off and in good health. On the surface, then, I had no excuse for my apathy and lost many friends because of it.

But the nightmare doesn't show itself on the surface; it sinks too deep for that.

I was so empty in myself that I couldn't bear to think about somebody else's problem; not even that of a close friend. My negative approach completely overruled any sensitivity I would otherwise have had. Once freed from my nightmare I recognised the effects it had created: that the mind, when in a depressed state, can go to town on our emotions and create negative reactions that might be groundless in reality.

If we hold onto negative thought or feeling, whether about a personal problem or about life in general, it isn't Truth we're holding onto, but the mind's distorted version of truth. Seen from another perspective and in a different light, the situation that initially caused the negative thought could also bring on a positive reaction.

For instance, consider the following scene: You're all ready to go on a family picnic, and it starts raining. What would your reaction be? Chances are you'd be irritated – the rain's going to spoil the day. I'm sure you know the feeling. It's a negative reaction to a perfectly natural everyday happening.

Now look at this: There's been a long dry spell during which water has been scarce. The heatwave and dust have become oppressive, and you cannot stand it any longer.

Then one day it unexpectedly starts to rain. You can't believe your eyes; it's like a miracle. You drop what you're doing, run outside and bask in the coolness of the rain on your face, absolutely exhilarated.

Do you see the difference? It was the same rain both times. What made it seem either negative or positive was your attitude towards the rain, not the rain itself. In either case, it was a natural enough reaction – anyone would feel that way. Nevertheless, it was still the mind's reaction that dictated whether you treated the occurrence as negative or positive.

The next time you're feeling low or moody, take a step back from the negativity and inspect your feelings with detachment.

This could be a turning point on your road to recovery.

No matter how despondent we may feel about a problem, it's merely our minds that have taken hold of the matter, dwelt on it and then pulled us down. When this happens we are prevented from recognising the reality and the truth which are always within reach: just outside the fortress, shining brightly.

All we have to do is acknowledge that this is so; then reach out to them with confidence. When we are feeling positive again, we'll be in a position to see that it was only the mind's deception at work.

This 'reaching out' is only speaking figuratively. In actual fact, we'd be reaching inwards to find sanctuary in our souls. The lower we feel, the greater we need to withdraw to it. When feeling low we're pretty withdrawn anyway; but it's usually the negative kind. By retiring to a place where there *is* no emptiness and loneliness, where we find peace and stillness within our own souls, in time we'll begin to witness Truth as it really is.

COPING WITH MOOD FLUCTUATIONS

When you are in a grumpy mood, everything you do is governed by your negative thoughts and emotions. For the duration of the mood, you are trapped within its confines and can think of nothing else. Whatever relates to it seems real to you, and helpful comments from others make little difference. Then unexpectedly, you come out of it. You might wake up feeling refreshed after a good night's sleep, or some interesting news brightens your day.

Alternatively, you may be a happy sort of person with no real worries to speak of. Then one morning, for no apparent reason you wake up in a bad mood, kick the dog, snap at the children and shout insults at other motorists.

But are you always able to put your finger on the reason for these fluctuating moods; or are they just there? Often they completely dominate once they've taken hold. The more other people try to cheer you up or tell you to 'snap out of it,' the worse you feel. The only way to get over a mood is to let it take its natural course and leave your system in its own time.

Yet, have you ever looked back over a day when you were low, or when a bad mood dominated you? All-consuming as it was, does it now appear to be nothing more than a flash in the pan, whether it lasted an hour, a day or a year? Was it actually of no permanent substance, and unrelated to the real world?

We can fashion moods into almighty barriers against the positive aspects of life. If we could prevent the barriers from existing at all and allow positive energy to flow freely through us, we might find a bright new world waiting to be explored. Then we would be able to build up immunity against those fluctuating moods; enabling us to recognise truth, and not be inhibited by everything that stops us from knowing harmony.

For some people, moods and low days are the exception, not the rule. They contentedly live their lives without too much worry. For others, though, moods seem to dominate and joy is rarely found. Everything goes against the grain, because they're so bogged down with problems that their outlook is habitually negative. To them, the negative world is the real world. There can be no other, for they've never allowed themselves to see it.

Yet, if something happens to lift them out of it, if only temporarily, everything appears in a different light.

The most enduring 'different light' is when we begin to awaken from the nightmare and find our own potential.

There are lots of things that may cheer us up and take us out of our moods; but they're usually just a quick fix. It's only the awakening of the human spirit, the inner 'lift,' that makes it enduring.

Taking hold of a dandelion by the root and removing it completely is what brings us out of the nightmare and into the light of day. When that occurs, the blessed sense of relief in discovering it's just been like a bad dream is quite beyond description.

The fluctuating moods you might be experiencing are just part of the nightmare. Be aware that the truth, the absolute 'Reality of Life,' is pulsating within your breast right now. As soon as you're able to recognise it you will begin to awaken.

At the moment you might still feel like saying, "How can any of this possibly relate to me?"

The answer is that it can relate to you, and it certainly *does* relate to you. This is clearly visible in the essence of life that's flowing through you.

Awaken from that nightmare of yours. Acknowledge the nothingness of these effects on your life, and start living. There is nothing in the world to stop you.

GETTING A GRIP ON ANGER

Our culture has always held the opinion that expressing anger is anti-social. To throw a paddy shows lack of control or aggression. To 'blow a fuse' implies an unstable mind.

This suggests that those still clinging to the view must have been born with an abundance of self-control, or have never had anything happen to cause them stress.

What's wrong with getting cross? It's a perfectly natural reaction that often gets results. And who's to say that in some cases expressing anger isn't in fact the correct action to take, despite what we've been taught?

To restrain anger, whether it's spontaneous or deeply rooted, adds to the build-up of tension. To let anger out is to release the safety valve and maintain a good balance.

There's a big difference, though, between getting angry and breeding anger.

If your children have been playing up all morning, you will probably reach a stage of zero tolerance; yet the only way you'll get through to them is by blowing that fuse. They're hardly likely to act upon, or even hear, your mild request of, "Now children, please be quiet."

Each situation varies and warrants a different approach. If on any occasion you feel justified in reading the riot act to the offenders, then who's to say it is wrong? Call it tough love, if you like. What's the alternative if less drastic action has been ineffective? Where's the harm in inflicting some 'fear of God' into them, or at least a healthy, yet caring fear of Mum or Auntie?

The danger to you and to all who are involved comes from harbouring the anger.

If, after having an assertiveness session, you can return to a reasonably calm state, then the little scene has probably been a lesson well learnt, both for them and for you. However, if the anger remains, you are in danger of allowing it to become ingrained over a period of time, and it will therefore be difficult to dispel.

The actions or reactions of others, emotional upsets, ill health, lack of sleep, stress, 'those difficult days' all affect our frame of mind and dictate what sort of mood we're likely to be in.

If the mind is tired and heavy the slightest thing may irritate or upset. The effort required for the simplest of chores seems like too much bother.

On the other hand, if the mind is light and spirits are high, then we aren't so quick to react. Physical tiredness is healthy and rewarding, and even the trickiest of daily tasks can seem straightforward.

Even though we're easily annoyed, a little comfort from within us can be a great morale-booster; helping to lift the mind so that worries don't sit so heavily on our shoulders. It enables us to throw the mind into neutral and thus deal with situations without stress or emotion.

Sometimes we're overwhelmed by a desire to just silence our minds. By sinking back into the comfort of our sanctuary and handing over all the strain, this can virtually be achieved. It's not necessary to withdraw from what we're doing; but merely give ourselves time to turn those thoughts inwards. To wait until a feeling of reassurance confirms that we've made contact, and then relax in the peace that this awareness brings.

RELEASE FROM JEALOUSY

Have you ever been jealous of somebody? Believe me, it can be a devastating experience: to feel resentment or envy towards another person, especially someone who is usually close.

Jealousy is the obsessive need to acquire something or somebody you don't have. You may envy a neighbour who wins the Lotto jackpot. You might be jealous of your buddy because you're besotted with his girlfriend. You might experience a sense of rivalry towards an older sister who is slender, vivacious and accomplished when you're cited as the opposite.

Envy, jealousy and rivalry: strong, malicious words that can be harmful, even to those we care about the most. Like most negative emotions, when we're in its grip jealousy controls our every mood and thought. We can make fools of ourselves and even break up friendships or marriages over something that in itself could be trivial.

But why should we feel the need to be jealous and controlling? Isn't it merely because we're dissatisfied with who we are or what we have?

While still in the nightmare, I was deeply envious of a colleague. She was expert in all that was expected of a woman of her times, and she was lively, pretty and witty to boot. The more often I compared myself with her, the more my self-esteem suffered.

Consequently, I withdraw into my fortress.

Not long afterwards, I went through my awakening from the nightmare, and in the process emerged from my fortress. Slowly I regained some self-esteem; to the extent that I was then able to view my jealousy from a new perspective. I still didn't excel in the same qualities as my colleague, but as time went by I found it didn't bother me anymore. I realised that although this woman was capable in her sphere, it didn't necessarily mean that mine should be the same as hers. The stronger I became in myself, the less jealousy I felt; all because I was now able to recognise my own identity and worth.

It's the emptiness inside that fosters jealousy. When we're complete and fulfilled our state of mind leaves no room for jealousy. We become content with who we are and what we have. Our potential, identity and worth are plain for all to see, especially ourselves.
   It is no longer hidden behind fortress walls.
   We still may not be excellent in our fields of endeavour, but we come to value the role we play in life, be it ever so humble. Then, once we have witnessed just what our capabilities and qualities are, the need to feel envy or resentment dissipates, and we come free of yet another burden.

BLAME, GUILT AND TEMPTATION

If somebody makes a grievous error, those affected by it focus on the offender and his misdemeanour, rather than on the fact that he has erred. The offender is deemed accountable, and whether intentionally or otherwise, the offence is held against him for a long time to come.
   How he feels about it doesn't seem to matter. Others are rarely interested in whether he's suffering remorse for what he has done; if was driven to it or has learnt an important lesson he will remember forever. They see only the offence and the blame that they attach to it.

Why do we feel the need to apportion blame when something goes wrong?

Are *any* of us entirely blameless – rushing to authorities or the media if we are slandered; the condemnation of those who infringe on our culture; the tittle-tattle behind each other's backs; the failure to seek out the truth? Do we have the right to condemn others for a mistake made today, when we're capable of doing the same tomorrow?

How do *we* feel when the shoe is on the other foot and we in turn are judged? We know the truth behind our errors; the human failings that lead to our undoing. And it hurts with the impact of a dropped bomb to realise that nobody else gives a damn.

Yet, whether we're offender or accuser, the reason we react this way is another result of those overwhelming odds. In this case, they could be in the form of human ego, pride, and the 'eye for an eye' attitude; not forgetting our feelings of guilt and self-doubt that can get in the way of forgiveness.

We can't help holding on to recriminations, though. We're still human with failings over which, whether we like it or not, we have little control. But with help from that which knows our real motives, we can reach a balance for living with mistakes or grievances – our own and those of other people. Then, when we've viewed them from a better perspective, we can send them to the 'recycle bin' in our minds.

We all slip up now and then. We're also capable of giving in to weakness. Some weaknesses are merely a nuisance, only affecting us. Others are branded criminal because they go against the grain of society. Yet behind every such act there is usually a deep-seated cause that we fail to acknowledge.

Possibly the 'offenders' are suffering inwardly from the sort of frustrations we all go through. The only difference now is that they've demonstrated frustration in a manner that Western society won't tolerate, whereas our own temptations might be more covert by nature.

However, this is only what the person *does*; it has nothing to do with who he *is*. It's a shame that who we are on the inside is still considered to be less important than what we get up to in the outside world.

The easiest way to find out who a person *is* has to be communication, and the only way to communicate on a universal level is with a smile.

A genuine, sincere smile between two people radiates a warmth that can only come from the intrinsic nature of those concerned. In most cases, whatever the background or antics of the individual, that nature is beautiful. When a person smiles, it doesn't seem to matter what he was up to beforehand – whether helping old ladies across the road or stealing from them. The antics of human beings reflect only their state of mind. They have nothing to do with the real identity beneath, which comes to the surface in a smile.

Years ago I worked with a local youth group on a Saturday night.

Some of the youngsters who attended had already been in trouble with the police, and were now considered to be no-hopers by a certain section of the community. Yet, after spending time amongst those sons or daughters of our townsfolk, I began to see a light that shone in them, revealing a depth and beauty I rarely saw amongst the 'respectable.'

Rough they sounded, rough they acted and rough they looked; but that was on the surface. Approached on their own terms, they were beautiful.

Not long after I started working with the group, a sullen-looking girl came along. As she walked close by, she glanced at me with a look that could kill. Instantly I knew my response was crucial to any further rapport I might have with her. So I smiled, though somewhat on edge as to how it would be received. In a flash, she responded; her sullen face transformed with a broad grin.

People like those youth group members might have a great deal of depth to them, yet this is rarely observed by the majority. Only their behaviour is noted.

It's a sad reflection on society that so much importance is placed on these antics, which are merely habits, peer group pressure, and temptations that cannot be resisted. But this is how society has evolved and for now we have to live with it.

The antics can't be ignored, though. Our standards and the law of the land rightly state that intervention might be needed. In days gone by we didn't care too much about the underlying nature, making it easier to condemn and ultimately charge the offenders.

Nowadays those in authority are more understanding.

There's a desperate need for people to get to know their own underlying nature: the intuitive side that's inclined to be overlooked. After all, this is the part of them which remains constant, whereas their superficial behaviour changes as they progress through life.

In this respect, a bit more leniency and understanding would go a long way with everyone; because few of us are completely free of guilt.

By understanding how we each tick, we're better able to disregard appearances and are therefore slower to judge or condemn. We can help ourselves and others to recognise and uplift the root cause of our troubles; thus providing the strength to resist further temptations.

The Importance of Trust

"I don't trust you." What a sad expression that is. What visions of despair and emptiness it conjures up. And what terrible harm it can do to all concerned.

Trust is an abstract emotion. It has neither donor nor recipient, but exists more as an 'air' between two people; a blanket of reassurance that envelops a situation. Yet, what a devastating effect it can have to know you're not trusted. How are you supposed to feel? How can you look the accuser in the eye again? It's as though all bonds of friendship suddenly crumple under the impact of those four little words, never to be restored.

Trust is as beautiful as love. Unspoken, trust doesn't need to be verified; it merely exists. It can, without thought or action, cement the bonds of marriage or friendship, within commerce or government, and even worldwide simply by being realised.

Trust has its source in the depths of the individual, and emerges from a bed that is stable and secure. When shared, it creates an ever-strengthening bond that's hard to break. But when the source is dried up; when the bed from which it should emerge is insecure and empty, there is created an unsettling gulf.

To feel trusted is to become trustworthy. Being made aware that another person trusts you allows you to reach out to the world.

The hardest of individuals are transformed by feeling trusted. Equally, those who are normally trustworthy can be devastated to realise they're *not* trusted.

Once I had a boss who didn't trust anyone. He'd been let down so many times that he distrusted most of his employees. This had a disturbing effect on the reliable workers, which led to a high staff turnover. I couldn't criticise him for his attitude, though. He had obviously been driven to bitterness over a long period of time. Nevertheless, his lack of trust took its toll. If only he'd been able to leave the past behind, the good workers in his employ would have given so much more for a positive attitude from him.

And doesn't this also apply to other relationships? Even the youngsters in the youth group behaved differently when they were shown a little trust. I believe this was because it ignited a positive spark in each of them, which gave them the incentive to venture out of their fortresses and reveal something of their true nature.

Trust is so important – from both perspectives. But it can only be brought about when there is a feeling of security within the people concerned.

And that sense of security can really only come from the one source.

THE USE OF WILLPOWER

We are urged to exercise willpower in many areas of life. To possess great willpower, according to some, is to be superior; to possess little is considered to be a weakness. However, believers in this approach have probably always had plenty of willpower, or they've never needed to tax themselves beyond the limit of their willpower.

Why should we be made to feel that lacking willpower is a weakness? Surely, having it in abundance is really no different from being physically strong, being good at sport, or choosing DIY over ready-made. It's more a question of personal values, abilities and interests; not one of moral fortitude.

All the willpower in the world is useless against odds with which we're unfamiliar or unable to cope. A usually stable and strong personality could easily be brought down to earth with a bump by a bewildering shock, and where would he be then? What would he have to fall back on and give him the strength he needs?

The possession of a certain amount of willpower or self-control is certainly desirable, but it's not the be-all and end-all. The motive in wanting to be strong is what counts and is likely to bring good results, not the amount of conscious effort we put into it. There are always situations that even the most assertive ego is unable to cope with, and to be put to the test is often what separates the men from the boys. And occasionally those who consider themselves to be the *men* find out they're really the *boys*.

It's all very well to adopt an attitude of, 'Say I can and you will.' First we need to have the confidence to say *I can* to begin with. Sometimes that plateau of incentive is so far out of reach that it seems impossible to even consider the possibility.

We can only exercise true willpower if something deep inside assures us we are able do it – no matter what it's in relation to. If the issue can easily be dealt with using willpower alone; that's good. When we're doubtful or reluctant, though, forcing it may lead to the reversal of whatever it is we've been willing ourselves to do.

For instance, if you've been trying without success to give up smoking, you might feel inadequate, resent comments from others and end up by smoking even more. Better it would be to acknowledge the fact that you're not yet ready to give it up; that the root cause behind wanting to smoke is still there; and that with a boost from your inner resources, somewhere in the near or distant future you will find the strength to do it. From a higher plateau of incentive, any such situation takes on a new perspective.

We can't make ourselves do *anything* that doesn't come easily. Getting out of a habit is no different from the principles involved when a child grows out of toys. It must be a natural progression, because forcing it will lead to frustration. We must be ready to make the transition, and the timing is something we can't consciously know – that is: when we're ready to move on, give up something or change our attitude and outlook. There has to be a sense of motivation before a move can be made, and if the individual concerned has not yet reached the plateau then this is unlikely to happen.

So what can we do when faced with a situation requiring willpower?

As many of life's problems seem too big to cope with, it is asking for trouble to attempt to overcome them without that inbred willpower – something we either possess or we don't.

Fortunately, assistance is never far away. We need only to connect with the power within that can cope with anything, and that is ready, willing and able to come to our rescue. It knows precisely when the time is right and the direction from which the help should come. And, in its own way, come hail or shine, with a shuffle or a clatter, it lets us know.

To illustrate this point, picture if you will the following scene:

You are sorting out the garden shed and come across an unusual seed. You haven't the faintest idea what type of plant it's from but your curiosity is aroused, and so you decide to propagate it. In time a green shoot appears: the plant is growing.

You're an experienced gardener who has watched many plants flourish and then die. You know this plant will be no different. There's a set pattern to the life of the plant, and it's only a question of time before each stage is reached and passed. But you're still in the dark as to the identity of the plant or how to care for it. Even though you want to, you can't begin to spray or prune, or follow any usual gardening procedures, until certain stages of growth are reached.

Time goes by and the mystery plant continues to grow; receiving the right treatment at the right time. Gradually you see it in its true light. The plant progresses through its cycle of life, and you are infinitely wiser for the experience.

Can you see that in a way we're both the seed and the gardener? Our growth in life takes a set course; this we already know – youth, maturity and old age. Yet we don't know what each intricate stage will be until we've reached and even passed it. Only the powers within us know when we're ready to 'prune,' overcome and move on. All we can do is observe and take note of the activity within.

When we're ready for the next step, whether it's giving up smoking, forgiving someone who has wronged us or discovering the meaning of life, we cannot make ourselves achieve these things until we've reached the right stage. It may be a question of hours or it may be many years.

Like the gardener getting to know his plant, we get to know ourselves, our strengths and even our weaknesses. We learn when to respond to motivation and where to leave well alone. Eventually we're able to recognise when we're at our various stages in life.

Willpower really counts for nothing. As a giant tanker is tossed like a matchstick on a stormy sea, so can the most powerful egos be brought down to size.

If your ego and willpower are in your opinion strong and stable: beware. If your ego and willpower in the eyes of the world leave much to be desired: fear not.

Don't be afraid to acknowledge in yourself that you have weaknesses, for you're in good hands. We're all in one way or another at the mercy of the stormy sea. But even the stormy sea is but a puppet in the hand that pulls the strings of the whole universe.

Look to the hand that pulls *your* strings and you can bring that willpower within your control.

LONELINESS AND INSECURITY

Loneliness and insecurity each contribute to our feelings of isolation: to our sense of detachment from others and from the world at large.

We can live alone or in a large family, and be lonely. We can be wealthy, waited on hand and foot, and still feel insecure. Both of these states are emotions. It's the *sense* of loneliness or insecurity, not the physical circumstance.

How we feel on the inside can even dictate whether we're lonely and insecure in the company of friends.

You may be with the same people two nights running; yet on the first night you're bubbling over, one of the crowd, thoroughly enjoying yourself; while on the second night you want to sit quietly to one side and observe, feeling isolated and alone.

When we're feeling lonely, it's not necessarily for other people or for compatible surroundings. Often it's because we're lacking a sense of identity. We don't really know ourselves. We're like strangers with ourselves, and may be hesitant when it comes to being alone; reluctant even to consider ourselves as a companion.

This is what we truly need: our own companionship.

We tend to alienate ourselves because we haven't yet recognised our true identity and all that it embraces. We're even reluctant to make a first move with ourselves. Given the chance, we would 'pass ourselves by on the other side of the street,' as we might with a stranger. The desire to escape our own company can be overpowering. Many of us fear we'll go crazy if we have to be alone for any length of time. Others hide within the fortress to avoid being hurt.

This is where a third party would be useful: someone to introduce us to ourselves; someone to help us recognise who we are and what our true capabilities are, but without the embarrassment of discussing it with another person.

Needless to say, the 'third party' is already there deep inside us; waiting for the opportunity to make itself known to us and help us get to know ourselves better.

We can be our own companion, our own best friend, our own wealth of security when we know ourselves. We can be locked inside our fortress and not feel cut off, or in a strange and foreign land and still feel at home. We can be clinging to a cliff face, amidst a pack of howling wolves or absolutely penniless and still feel secure.

TAKING THE EASY WAY OUT

This runs on from lack of inner security. It could apply to anyone at any age.

Sometimes we're so unsure of ourselves that in difficult circumstances the easiest solution is the one that comes most readily to mind. For instance, comfort and pleasure are easier to live with than anxiety or pain. Pleasant tastes such as sweet, juicy and tasty are easier to consume than bitter or bland. It's easier to watch television than read a book, to download a movie than take the family out to the cinema; to ride on the treadmill than go for a walk, buy produce from the supermarket than grow and dig your own; to promise to do something than actually do it; win money than earn it. And it's much easier to get cross than to exercise a little patience.

We give in out of habit, or because we're not used to doing things the hard way. That's understandable, though. So much is made easy for us these days.

Even in the animal world the easy way is taken. Go over to your window and look out. Are there any birds on the lawn? If so, what are they doing? Rummaging around for worms, no doubt; and happily, too. Now scatter some bread and watch what happens. Are those sparrows you see, or have they morphed into vultures? What a difference. Those benign little creatures, foraging around for food, have suddenly gone mad.

Easy pickings for the taking or grabbing; for fighting or for killing: That's how it finishes up occasionally, isn't it?

Do *you* sometimes take the easy way out? If you're not sure, the following may ring a bell:

A father is irritated with his teenage daughter for spoiling his afternoon nap. He takes the easy way out by giving her some money and packing her off to the mall with a friend. He could have sat down with her, talked about what might be troubling her, encouraged her with a hobby or maybe suggested, "Let's go and visit Grandma;" something which would have involved them both. But this would have been too much effort, and these days he's not used to making an effort where his daughter is concerned. As it stands, with daughter off to the shopping mall – or wherever she really goes – the problem is only temporarily solved, and will be just the same tomorrow, and the day after that.

Whenever we 'take the easy way out' we're deceiving ourselves. The more frequently we put off, avoid, escape and ignore potential problems, the harder it is when we're obliged to face them. Because that's how it invariably ends up: we have to face our problems.

Yet, the reason we take the easy way out in the first place is probably because we don't know what else to do, and wouldn't be motivated to do it, anyway. We may have already tried other ways without success, and given up. Or perhaps we just don't want to get involved.

But what if, at the onset of a scenario like this, the solution came effortlessly to mind? What's more, if we actually felt like having a crack at it, wouldn't that make a difference? All those weeks, months or years of putting off the slowly worsening inevitable would have been avoided. The relentless build-up of complacency that frequently accompanies this situation wouldn't be there at all.

This may sound far-fetched, but it's not. It's within the grasp of anyone willing to give it a try. There's no such thing as a quick fix; it's all very much a gradual progression from not caring to instantly knowing what to do. But if you're the sort of person who's inclined to take the easy way out and now regret it, remember inspiration is only a heartbeat away.

EVERYDAY NEEDS AND FEELINGS

This is something we might associate with eating and sleeping, and so on; yet it's far more inclusive than that. Each thought or emotion is caused both by the desire for a need to be satisfied and the feeling we get when that need has been met. The body and mind seem to tell us what they want, and we are compelled to respond.

A kitten will cry pitifully if it is hungry, but when its need for food has been satisfied, then it purrs.

One of my own cats has the right idea. In the main she keeps herself to herself, bothering no one. Yet when she recognises a need she goes all out to make sure it is met. She pesters and pesters until she's fed or let out or cuddled, and once that's done she clears off to wherever it is she goes and whatever it is she does. She seems to regard it as a right that her needs be met, and whatever the object of her need – food, drink or a comfy chair – then it is her right to be given her share.

Similarly, we each recognise a need and in the main know where to obtain it. If we are cut off from the source of supply or if there is no chance of the need being met, the mind doesn't concede, 'Alright, we're out of luck today so let's forget it.' Instead, it builds up resentment towards whatever is causing the deficit and craves satisfaction even more.

A child may moan to his mother, "I'm hungry;" only to be told, "You'll have to wait for tea." Does that make the hunger go away?

It's impossible to ignore the signals that our minds and bodies are sending out.

Comments from others are sometimes made, such as 'get a grip,' 'control yourself;' 'pull yourself together,' or even, 'forget about it.' But as we're not complete masters of our own minds, there are occasions when this can't be achieved. Surely we're not meant to 'forget about it' like that. Just as the cat knows she needs food, something inside of us – even if we don't recognise it – understands that we have a particular need at a specific time.

It is the need, not the person, that demands redress and when it's not satisfied, aggravation sets in.

Isn't it obvious from the sad state of Western society that our intrinsic needs are *not* being met? Is this really our fault?

I would say, no. If anything, it is mainly the fault of our inherited civilisation for becoming blind to its own needs and for ignoring the alarm signals.

The 'something' inside us that declares our needs also has the wherewithal to placate them. Up until now, our ignorance of what makes us all tick has impeded that power from guiding us in the right direction. With proper understanding of the laws that operate within the human mind and body; those same principles that function throughout the whole universe – we could be led to the wellspring for all our needs.

I believe that only by having our various needs met in an appropriate fashion can we fully develop as complete human beings. By 'listening' to our intuition and following the natural laws that flow through us, this could well be accomplished.

FINDING OUR NICHE IN LIFE

Have you ever felt more comfortable living in one house, street or township than another; or perhaps preferred one place of employment over any of the others? If so, do you ever wonder why this might be?

Generally, we find it hard to settle within just one situation, for human beings seem to be restless by nature. These days we even travel to the ends of the earth looking for our 'true home.' It's as though we are searching for the ideal setting, and until it's found we can be restless and undecided.

There appears to be some kind of niche that each of us fits into, and we can spend a lifetime searching for it. Some find it, some don't. Job-hunting, partner-finding or looking for a new place to live are all part of this.

During our search there will come a time when we must take some giant steps. These may be made confidently and with enthusiasm, or shakily with fear and trembling. There's the feeling of being thrown in at the deep end when a student leaves school and faces the unenviable task of finding a job; or the excitement of a young woman who's soon to be married. Then there's the anticipation of moving into a new home; the physical, emotional and financial upheaval of a marriage or partnership break up. And, more commonly, there's the heartbreak of leaving home and family to live in a foreign land.

It's hard to envisage what's going to happen once we've taken these steps.

We might put them off because we worry about making the change, thinking only of the pitfalls. Or we might rush headlong into them without due consideration, imagining the whole thing to be a bed of roses. On the other hand, we can be brave, acknowledge that the step must be made, and allow our support system to take over; then calmly step up to the edge of now – and jump. With guidance from our intuition, there is little reason to be apprehensive. The closing of any door may be the end of one phase in our lives, but it's just the start of another. And when we do open the next door, sooner or later the way will be revealed.

This support system: our intuition, our spirit, knows that we must take those steps, just as it knows the buds open in spring and that our planet must spin on its axis. It never fails such manifestations that depend on it. Why then should we think it might fail us? It won't. It is utterly reliable.

In effect, it's the only benefactor this side of eternity that's completely dependable.

If you are happy with your job, your home, or life in general, then there's no dilemma.

However, if these aspects of life begin to grind or seem meaningless to you, they can become very hard to live with, and leave you with a feeling of restlessness. The reason for this feeling could be that your instincts are nudging you to move on with your life. After all, how else could you know?

When this happens, you need to discern what is real and meaningful, and where your future may lie. Once you've made this distinction, opportunities may well begin to open up. Responding is like pushing over a domino: it can start a chain reaction that heads us off in the right direction, even if we don't know what that direction might be. The difficulty is in summoning up the courage to push over that first domino. By hesitating, a valuable opening could be missed.

However, there is also the possibility that we're so consumed by our dilemma that we are oblivious to all that is real and meaningful right now.

Sometimes we're blind to the good things that exist in our lives and environment, because it's human nature to constantly seek and search elsewhere.

As the saying goes, 'The trouble with not knowing what you want is that you don't know you've got it when you get it.'

So if you're restless, take care that what you're seeking isn't already staring you in the face. Hold back from your desire for a moment and let your intuition be your guide. You might find out that today's the day to push over the first domino – or you may realise you don't need to push any over at all.

If our ideal situation isn't immediately forthcoming, or the step we're anxious to take doesn't show itself straight away, then we can be very impatient.

For example, an A-grade school leaver goes job hunting but can't find a suitable position. His father is annoyed in equal measure with the son and with society, as though it's his right that their offspring should find a career-of-a-lifetime straight away. What neither would realise is that the niche the son is to occupy could have nothing to do with his qualifications or the job market, and may not make itself known for many years.

The result is that the son gives up hope, pressure from the father ruins their relationship, and the entire scenario gets out of hand.

'Now if not sooner' is our motto these days. We seem unable to allow one day to follow-on from the other, one domino to fall after the last, and just see what turns up. We spend hours checking the want ads, surfing the Net or pacing the streets. All this achieves is a waste of time, energy and money; which we may not have to spare.

If we could only stop trying to make everything happen by our own conscious effort, and allow ourselves to be motivated along the right channels, we would get on much better. We'd find that ideal job; or at least, something that suits for the time being. We'd be guided to the partner, home or country that will satisfy the nesting instinct. The giant step would be taken with a minimum of torment.

Alternatively, if our true niche in life is where we are right now, then we've merely failed to recognise it. With that same trust we can gradually alter our attitude, until one day we find ourselves at peace in the same situation that once caused the feeling of unrest.

Sometimes we have an idea of what our perfect situation should be: a desire that remains in the back of the mind year after year. Yet because of current circumstances we're unable to follow-up on it.

If you are aware of something deep inside, or are motivated along a certain line but feel you can't pursue it, don't dismiss it out of hand. Your inner resources may be quietly setting the course for things to come. Keep the channels open, and watch what happens. If something feels right, there's every possibility it *is* right. You never know, one day your wildest dreams may come true.

A comment I once heard suggested, 'we appreciate the good things of today when we realise they're a part of dreams started yesterday.'

Our continual longing is not merely a human heritage; its roots go much deeper than that. In fact, it is the pining of the soul for freedom from restriction, and for the resurgence of its own identity. Once that identity has been established, there is no longer any need to aimlessly wander the face of the planet, because the soul, and therefore the individual, has found its niche. When this happens, the searching and the desiring are over; for we are home.

If we allowed ourselves more freedom to do what our intuition is urging us to do, we might find ourselves at peace with the things we're obliged to do, as well.

PHYSICAL CONTACT AND LOVE

One of the strongest drives in humankind is desire. The drive is created by a build-up of pressures, by the inability to derive fulfilment from our everyday lives, or by the natural human need to give and receive affection. And one of the most effective ways of dealing with such pressures is a romantic liaison with someone we love.

Our physical needs are varied and complex, and cannot be generalised. In essence, each person's needs, with their intuition guiding them, should be free to deal with these emotions in their own way. However, danger lurks and the trouble starts when other people are involved or affected; such as unwilling and forceful partners, conflicting habits, standards or cultures, and the spread of diseases.

The end result of this is so often emotional chaos and hardship; not forgetting depression, promiscuity and life-threatening infections.

Maintaining a healthy love life is never hopeless; risky maybe, but not hopeless. All we need to do is open up, so that our inner resources are better able to select and then maintain a good, healthy balance.

Human relationships can rarely be described as plain sailing. To give rein to a guiding light that has everybody's interests at heart is the only course of action that leads to a stable existence alongside our partners.

The concerns we have about personal relationships are understandable: they involve some powerful drives that can lead to trouble. Yet we Westerners are notoriously standoffish when it comes to physical contact in general.
…Why should this be?
After all, we fondle pets, cuddle children and embrace our families; but for some reason, apart from shaking hands when we meet, or when the team hugs on a football pitch, we find it difficult to touch anyone else. Yet an affectionate hug, whether to the opposite sex or our own, can do as much good as a pick-me-up. A hand placed on the shoulder is a wonderful source of comfort. In being reserved towards one another we deprive ourselves of both the giving and receiving of affection.

Although the need for physical contact is part of our make-up, there are many people who are unaffected by such pressures. Somehow they've reached a stage within themselves where there's no longer any emptiness, and therefore no longing. To them physical pleasures enhance an already fulfilling life – like savouring the icing on top of a rich fruit cake, rather than seeking nourishment from the cake itself. Desire for fulfilment is no longer an issue for them.

Wouldn't this be the ideal state for the rest of us? Wouldn't a welcome alternative to seeking satisfaction for our longings be to avoid them altogether? For the root cause behind our needs to be uplifted so that we're more secure, less lonely and therefore happier in ourselves? We could then go on to savour this aspect of life instead of depending on it.

We talk about 'love;' but what do we mean by that? The word is open to several interpretations. We can love a husband or a daughter, a friend or a pet; a celebrity, even. All these forms of love manifest differently.

Yet the underlying 'love' is like a common thread that unites them all and comes from deep within.

It's the emotion that usually goes with it, which renders the various forms of love different and is responsible for so much possessiveness, heartbreak and jealousy.

But this isn't really 'love.'

Love should be a beautiful expression of Self rather than a clinging, needy desire. In the purest sense of the word it is the grace to share and enhance. It's knowing when to give, knowing where to withhold and knowing when to let go. A selfish love that demands gratification with little regard for the other is merely lust. This is sad because it means that the individual lacks personal fulfilment, and acts from a sense of want. Others who consider themselves to be 'in love' may become emotional or obsessed.

These reactions stem from our hesitation, conditioned by inbred culture, to respond to our intuition; normally and naturally.

The close relationship between partners isn't just sex, it is an act of complete love, and one is lacking without the other. Love without sex leads to frustration; sex without love can result in bitterness. In its completeness, love is the most beautiful experience of human physical life. In its completeness it leads to peace and harmony.

To live without a feeling of love, either giving or receiving, is to feel empty inside; for love is the essence of life and nobody can exist in fullness without it.

Ideally, everybody should be able to partake in such giving and receiving, but this is not the case. Some people lead solitary lives, or bitter and unhappy lives, because love doesn't flow from them and to them as it should. It's there, though; love is most definitely there. Every so often in the 'meanest' individual a spark of love shines through a crack in the fortress wall, as I saw in our youth group kids. The effect of this can be explosive. Love is the essence of life, and life is constantly flowing through us. When there's no person or pet to share our lives, we're still able to feel the love within us if we keep open the channel to our soul centre, and allow it to emerge.

Love would still course through each of us, and the effect it would have on our lives would be just as beneficial as the love of a whole family.

We talk about the need to 'love yourself.' I believe what this means is to feel that love in our hearts. We would then need no other person to fill an emotional void. It would be replenished from deep within our being.

Once our souls are replenished, the love will begin to seep out to others of its own accord.

MARRIAGE

The institution of marriage has been around for many centuries. Whether it's essential or unnecessary that we marry will probably be open to conjecture for many more to come. Yet one thing is certain: the reasons for marrying today are far different from those of years gone by.

Every generation down the centuries has held different opinions concerning marriage: arranged marriages to keep the family name going, marriage for money, marriage to legitimise sex, marriage because was expected of us, and no doubt many more.

What, then was the original or underlying reason behind this time-honoured institution?
How about, the bringing together of two people who love and respect each other; who know without a shadow of doubt that they are meant for each other, and who recognise deep down inside that they are as one?
It sounds idealistic, but isn't this how marriage should be, and not for any other reason?

Even in this era of anything goes, it is still considered the norm that an engaged couple will sooner or later get married. After the honeymoon they tentatively explore different aspects of their new way of life; then discover that the honeymoon is soon replaced by the mundane. Taken by surprise, they can't understand why their union is not developing as harmoniously as they once assumed. Without training in the difficult art of marital partnership, and with no respected mentor to advise, morale begins to slip.
Over a period of time their marriage deteriorates, and the rest is common knowledge.
Is this marriage? It's marriage for our modern times, for sure. The independence that so many girls aspire to and the deliverance from being 'left on the shelf;' the macho image so important to the male of our species, are often swept aside and replaced by a sense of entrapment, of inadequacy and of confusion.
...And then there are the children.

Obviously, not all marriages are like this. Some work well. There are many couples who are ideally suited and are the envy of all around – or maybe the partners just happen to be compatible. But don't the relevant statistics speak for themselves? For a few decades now, at least one in three marriages has ended in divorce.

If it's security they are looking for, or independence and love, then surely the institution of marriage is not the right answer. In fact, it's probably unwise to enter into such a binding relationship without an absolute conviction that this person is the right one; not for what each can get out of the other, but for what they can mutually share. If there's an element of doubt in the mind of either partner, then the answer should be, "No;" or at least, "Give me time;" as much as is necessary to establish whether the partners really are compatible. Never mind pressure from friends, family or your own emotions. Marriage is a legal and in some cases a lifetime commitment.

Living together, once frowned upon, is nowadays an acceptable form of partnership and is a good way of getting to know your intended. But it's inadvisable to sign on the dotted line unless something inside you is 100% certain. Freedom is of supreme importance; once lost it's hard to regain. When you are in an unhappy marriage, especially with children involved, it's too late for regrets.

Marriage is like buying an item with a non-returnable sticker: once bought, you can't take it back for a refund without a lot of bother.

Security, love and independence are not there to be snatched when we can; they are, or can be, instilled inside each of us without any need to include someone else. They can be touched and realised at a moment's notice, just by turning to that core within, which is quietly pulsating inside even the unhappiest of people; sending out signals to comfort and guide us in the important decisions we often need to make. With this backing, there is no urgency to find our soul mate. And even if we are well into our thirties, fifties or eighties before we find someone, the fact that we haven't yet met the ideal partner should not cause concern. There are plenty more fish in the sea to be going on with.

So much frustration is caused by unsuccessful marriages, whatever the reason for their existence in the first place. Many of us consider it out of the question to start seeking a more suitable partner; at least until the fledglings have left the nest, or some other family situation has been resolved. Habits can be very hard to change, and unhappy wives or husbands would rather remain in surroundings with which they are familiar, than risk the insecurity and upheaval involved in starting again.

Yet, even an upheaval of this magnitude needn't be a lonely experience, with the reassurance that all will be well coming from deep within.

It's so easy to react impulsively where relationships are concerned; either in acquiring a partner or in letting go of one. As with most things, time and patience are of the utmost importance. Allowing things to take their natural course may seem impossible, but very often it's the only answer of benefit to all.

Nobody really wants to hurt others, do they? Isn't it only done out of desperation?

The natural course – our path in life that's driven by the same force which moves whole galaxies – will also channel us in the right direction, if given the chance.

THE ROLE OF PARENTHOOD

What an impressive title. It sounds like being a parent is a privilege; and indeed it is. Even so, many parents, although devoted to their kids, would like to have a break from them at times.

Parenthood is often approached with pre-conceived ideas from those closest to us: from prospective grandparents waiting for the young marrieds to announce their 'news;' from doting relatives anxious to see the continuance of the family line; the anticipation of offspring to follow in father's footsteps. All of these are attitudes inherited from previous generations.

Surely, once the excitement of a new birth fades, the role of parenthood is yet another 'job' that has to be undertaken.

When anyone takes on a form of employment there is usually a certain amount of in-house training before they can begin their work: a period of supervision until the job is well-learnt. After that, it's a matter of following routines and gaining experience.

But what training do we give a couple expecting their first child? Little enough on the art of bringing up children and being good parents.

Admittedly, we do get start-up advice from relatives and the visiting nurse; or from books, television and the Internet. This suffices until things begin to go wrong: when a situation develops for which an acceptable solution is not found from the mother-in law, a suitable website or a child welfare group. Then frustration sets in. Not knowing what to do, we can become irritated with our partner and the child: the beginnings of a crisis or an ongoing habit.

When my first child was born, I easily became flustered, and quickly ran out of ideas for pacifying a tiny baby who seemed to be constantly crying. The visiting nurse said, "Do what you feel like doing." How could I tell her that the only thing I felt like doing was to run away and not come back? Having been assured that all mothers experience a maternal bond with their first baby, I felt terrible when I realised that this 'post-natal' mother didn't.

We are somehow expected to know straight away what to do for our children. It would not occur to us otherwise. But few instinctively do – with the firstborn, anyway.

If the baby is what we call 'good,' there's no problem. Later on if the toddler, and then the child, does what we want him to do, and eventually turns out the way we think he should turn out, we cope admirably and enjoy the experience. But when our offspring becomes independent, refusing to accept regular feeds as a new baby or parental advice as a teenager, then parents can be at a loss to know what to do for the best.

And there are many phases of childhood to be coped with.

Our natural instincts and intuition are presumed to come to the fore in times like these. Yet they can be so blocked by the burdens of parenthood and other pressures that they can't get through to show us how to do it. Birds and animals manage their offspring all right. Mind you, they have the edge on us. Once their youngsters are old enough they nudge them out of the nest. If we humans instinctively knew what to do, we would cope so much better.

It's not that we don't care, but that we often become overwhelmed. In frustration, we finish up by taking either drastic action or the easy way out: anything but the best way.

Parents can become completely bogged down by the demands of their offspring. In our culture the era of the integrated family is long over. These days, young couples leave their home environment far more frequently than in previous generations. There are no built-in babysitters, and both parents are overloaded with work or domestic responsibilities. Husbands are moved around in their jobs, and wives become isolated from relatives.

Children too often don't have anyone to relate to apart from their friends online. As a result, parents and children are in danger of becoming utterly frustrated with each other and with family life in general.

It's a vicious circle, which gets no one anywhere.

The key to successful family living in these circumstances would have to be patience and understanding, only we can become so snowed under that this seems impossible.

We need to try and understand how each of us feels, and be mindful of changing feelings; especially those of young parents. These may be feelings such as why we lash out when we do; why we sink into the doldrums when we do, and most especially, why we sometimes feel a need to break away or drown our sorrows. But if this isn't possible, then maybe the mere acceptance that this is how we are just now.

It's not that Mrs Brown is trying to belittle Mr Brown, but more likely the stressed and frantic young mother is defending herself against an equally stressed-out husband. And it's not Teenage Daughter Smith holding a grudge against Mother Smith, but pressured offspring fighting for freedom from a dominant parent – or maybe it's the other way round. We can become so hemmed-in, parents and children alike, that we are unable to recognise what's essential to help us get through. Instead, all we do is turn on each other.

Yes, patience, understanding and the acceptance of everyone's needs are the only way forward in surviving the difficult role of parenthood.

As parents, the initiative has to be ours. These days a child won't take any notice of something the parent isn't prepared to put into practice. And that could be anything from encouraging good behaviour in the little ones to administering tough-love when they're older.

All we need to do, when words or actions fail us, is to root out that intuition. To stop, listen and then respond when we are prompted from deep within. If the unifying factor between all people was allowed to lend a hand, then the rough times in parenthood would be so much smoother, the right course of action made evident, and we would be able to cope.

THE COMPLEXITY OF YOUTH

Our youth of today is a much-maligned entity; but then so was the youth of every generation that preceded it.

What is it about youth that makes it what it is; or rather what it appears to be: a rebellious, apathetic, arrogant section of society intent on defying the norm? And what happens to youth when it ceases to be youth – when it grows up?

Let's do some investigating:

The majority of us grow up in a family environment. We receive very little training for the role of parenthood, so when difficulties arise it's tempting for first-time parents to take the easy way out.

Again, this is not so much because they don't care, but because they don't know how to deal with off-the-wall youngsters.

Parents forget very easily what it's like to be young, and see the children through their own insular adult eyes. Children have never had the experience of being an adult and have no idea about adult problems or how their parents think and feel.

So there's a shortage of understanding right from the start.

Irrespective of a child's age, whether infant or young adult, there are bound to be situations where the parents' lack of insight leads to misunderstanding.

This is where the trouble starts.

Many parents for whom the difficulties are a new experience just don't know how to cope. So they take the line of least resistance by telling their child to shut up, go watch a movie, do as you're told, 'ask your mother,' and so on. The real reasons behind the difficulties are forced back into him and there they remain hidden; for the time being, anyway. If this builds up over years, it is easy to see how the suppression of feelings might become unbearable for a child. Inside him are a host of pent-up frustrations, along with his usual 'growing pains': wild emotions, physical changes, peer pressures and expectations, and the natural desire to do-your-own-thing. In the end, he doesn't know if he's coming or going. Nobody listens to him, and his parents don't seem to care.

...So what does he do?

He establishes his ego as a force to be reckoned with, but really it's a camouflage: a fortress wall that he hides behind, because he cannot bear the hurt he feels inside.

Children instinctively like to experiment with their lives. Too often, though, they cannot do this because authority or the latest trends lure them away from such instincts. Older people get in the way or aren't there when needed. Their inner confidence is instilled and grows when a good balance of freedom and guidance is offered and they learn intrinsically what life is all about, rather than from alien standards that beguile or oppress them.

Working with the youth group was a good education for me. I was able to observe how the youngsters changed from week to week. There seemed to be a pattern:

At first, new members would behave as they were expected to behave: insolent, disruptive, often crafty; displaying those negative labels so frequently attached to the young. As the weeks went by and they began to accept that the grown-ups posed no threat to their freedom, they started to settle down and be themselves. In many cases being 'themselves' was very different from the concept others had of them.

Their underlying nature began to surface.

While the teenagers were there, few restrictions were placed upon them, over and above acceptable behaviour. For those brief periods each week the pressure they were under in the outside world was lifted.

Had we been able to continue the youth group, we would have grown and no doubt watched our charges grow, too. But we had to close down because, despite efforts to gain support from their parents and the local community, nobody was interested enough to help. We got the impression from the adults that these sons and daughters of our town were considered a race apart and too difficult to deal with.

The stage of development we call 'youth' is only one of many that we go through. Youth has to – and does – grow out of youth, just as a child must grow out of toys and adults will eventually grow out of status symbols. It's all a very natural process. But for some reason, where youth is concerned we fail to recognise it.

This is the most difficult stage of development in the whole of our lives. We are under pressure from school and home; peer groups and trends. Our bodies, our outlook on life, our social challenges and acceptances are all changing. We have so little experience of the intrinsic values in life that we can't see wood for trees. Yet all we get from those who are supposed to be 'older and wiser' is criticism.

When the child or teenager is continually prevented from discovering his inner potential, he reaches a stage where his hackles rise out of sheer frustration. He thumbs his nose or worse at his nearest and dearest, at those who have authority over him, and at anyone who's getting in his way; and he rebels.

As he outwardly rebels, he also inwardly withdraws: back into his fortress, whether or not assisted by drugs. Outside pressures are not part of the insular world he creates for himself. He sees stability only within that fortress. And even though the young person still longs for freedom, the incessant pressure he's under means he can make no headway. The outside world is alien to him. This conditioning escalates with each successive generation, and youth continues to rebel.

Those identities on whose shoulders the future of our world rests are branded for life – or at very least, for the time being.

But what happens to them when in the fullness of time they're no longer young people – when they become adults living in an adult world? They don't also cease to exist as personalities; neither do they always see the folly of their ways and reform.

...So where do they go, and what do they do?

In many cases they give up the fight for personal freedom and are swept into the fast-flowing torrent of the rat race; not because they don't want to resist anymore, but because they don't know what else to do.

Consumed by the outer world, there they lose the incentive to develop their individuality. They may find jobs and careers, get married and have children. Or, sadly, live off the dole, get hooked on drugs or alcohol, and even start down the slippery slope towards crime. Either way, a mundane routine, which may last the rest of their lives, is set in motion.

Vibrant youth is lost and gone forever, or so it would seem. Freedom of self-expression, the wonder of young love and youthful exuberances of life; they are all gone. In their place: the rat race, the weekend footy match, the social climbing ladder; domestic arguments, law-breaking, illicit drugs and these days: binge drinking.

Contentment in them is rare.

If we could wind back the clock, is there any way we might prevent this downward spiral? Let's take a look:

The child is becoming repressed. Right; hold it there. Firstly: no more repression. A little consideration is needed for the child's plight – and also for the parents' difficulties. Both need help, but where from? Advice is often a bitter pill to swallow; especially if you're so fed up you don't really give a damn.

So much for that. Nobody else is likely to get through that fortress wall; either the parent's or the child's. The only way to infiltrate it is by recognising the truth and beauty of what lies within each other's fortresses, and to coax it out.

There is still the goodness and beauty of youth in all of us, whatever our age and the density of our fortress walls. It's only hidden; not destroyed.

By recognising our potential and allowing our intuition to emerge, we're in a better position to understand what's going on and to do something about it.

Everybody would like to feel they are loved. We all need a sense of identity and belonging. Whatever our age, none of us can live a complete life without them. By allowing these to develop early, with inspired guidance, there's no reason why we should not live a full and happy life within our families and within the community.

ENCROACHING OLD AGE

When I was little, I remember my mother celebrating her 30th birthday. In my juvenile innocence I thought she was old. More recently I had an acquaintance 100 years of age, and she was youthful in comparison with others much younger. Age, therefore, is relative. However, of one thing we can be certain: in the natural scheme of things, sooner or later the majority of us will become old.

A child might look at his grandparents and think of them as being old, but it's unlikely he would contemplate the fact that *he* will ever be old. Nevertheless one day, barring misfortune, it will happen.

Beating the ageing process is big business these days. Face lifts, anti-wrinkle creams and injections; multi-vitamin supplements together with diet and exercise regimes – all promise to make us last longer, look younger. Even so, the decades eventually catch up and we realise, much to our dismay, that we've joined the ranks of the aged.

So what happens then? What happens when we finally have to accept that the ravages of time have overtaken us? That we're likely to succumb to one or more of the many degenerative complaints associated with old age: a stroke, a heart attack, arthritis or a hip replacement.

The onset of Alzheimer's disease may send our relatives into a tailspin, and we wake up one day to find we've been moved into a rest home or enrolled at a day-care facility.

Plenty of money can be made out of the elderly, and many families find themselves with no other choice than to place elderly relatives into care.

For instance, an elderly woman, perhaps only recently widowed, may be lucky enough to have her family close by who lovingly cater for her every need. Or, she may be left on her own, with her family settled in another town and with no encouraging prospects. The local retirement village would then be a viable option. A devoted daughter may desperately want to care for her mother at home, but cannot cope with Mum's needs as well as those of her family. Or, a busy son finds caring for an ailing parent too stressful to deal with, and reluctantly absorbs the expense of residential care.

Whether we're the aged or a carer of the aged, life can become very difficult when old age enters into the equation, and we can be left wondering which way to turn. The independence of both the older person and the carer; so strong and vital only a short while ago, seems to be swept aside when old age rears its head. Instead, we find ourselves with no choice but to follow dictates that are suddenly thrust upon us.

It goes something like this: "Mother cannot possibly cope on her own, so I've got no alternative but to take her in, even though I have a young family, a husband and a much needed part-time job."

Or maybe it's a case of, "I'm too old and infirm to look after myself any more. I know I need help, but don't want to impose upon my family who are already struggling to make ends meet and take care of themselves."

And then there's, "It's so demoralising being like this. I'm not the person I used to be. I've lost my looks, my figure, my health and my independence. What do I have to live for now?"

There's no escaping the inevitability of the above, but as with so many unavoidable phases in life, they can either depress us or they can enrich us; they can be resisted or taken in our stride.

Old age can be a time of joy or a time of sorrow; or maybe a combination of both. If you are either the older person or the carer, you always have a choice. You can allow the situation to get you down, or seek guidance from deep within for all the problems you're envisaging.

As the carer, you would need to take regular time out for yourself, if only snatched moments of peace and quiet, to make your life and that of others involved a little easier. If you concentrate on *being* while you are doing all these added essentials, you will remain centred and therefore comparatively free in yourself; swimming strongly with the emotional current instead of allowing it to drag you along with it.

Inspiration from within would show you the help you need. With its guidance you could meet the person who will next assist you, or you might notice an advert for a disability aid you're after. It could give you the overtime you need to pay some medical bills – or even allow you a modest win on Lotto. It will definitely give you a few unexpected and welcome moments to pause, relax and once again turn within to that great source of all your needs. Then, rested and revitalised, you can tackle the next phase of your day.

Old age doesn't have to be lonely and depressing. The most helpful carer of all, your inner Self, is aware of your situation and all your requirements. It will comfort you and provide for you in your times of greatest need.

CHRONIC, DEBILITATING AND TERMINAL ILLNESS

It is said that 'on this side of heaven, life is but a training ground for higher things;' and nothing can be more testing than debilitating illness.

When you are well and happy with much to anticipate, the prospect of the many years ahead is very pleasing to contemplate. You are free to go where you will and do as you wish. Beyond the need to exercise caution there is nothing to hold you back. However, if you injure yourself, even something as minor as a cut finger, it's both annoying and can restrict your activities.

Badly sprain your ankle and you're off your feet for a week. While you're recuperating it seems as though you're repeating the same boring day over and over again; until at long last it heals and you're back to normal.

Even the most common ailments can immobilise you. Think how many people are kept off work when 'flu is around, and how debilitating recurrent migraines can be.

A multitude of physical complaints can prevent us from getting on with life. For most of us, though, these are only temporary setbacks. Sooner or later the ankle injury heals, and we usually get over our colds and 'flu with a minimum of fuss. Quite quickly we're able to get back to normal.

If surgery is involved, normality is achieved after an appropriate period of recuperation.

But what of those for whom the illness or complaint isn't temporary: people whose injuries are so severe that the victim is now a paraplegic? Or maybe someone who's been diagnosed with a condition like multiple sclerosis? Those vibrant people who know without a shadow of doubt that from this day forward their lives will never be normal again.

Imagine what it is like to find out that you will never walk again, that you have an incurable, or even a terminal condition. How would you cope with such a revelation?

...Or is it something you already have to cope with?

It's hard for those of us whose bodies are in good order and functioning normally to comprehend how it must be for those whose bodies are not. Some things you can only understand if you experience them for yourself.

All we can do is empathise, and offer whatever help is acceptable and within our capability. We may not be able to walk in those people's shoes, but one thing we *can* do is imagine what it must be like: to sense their physical pain, emotional trauma, or despondency.

Some able-bodied people can't cope with another person's disability. If someone in the family is paralysed in a car accident, the response from relatives can range from instant support to never being there when they're needed. The trauma of accident and illness affects not only the victim, but also everyone connected with the victim. People's strengths and limitations vary, and a major crisis can reveal them for all to see. You may find it easy to be supportive, or you may be the one who finds it hard.

Many of us fear hospitals and disabilities in general. This isn't something to be ashamed of, nor is it weakness. It's yet another characteristic over which, on our own, we have little control.

If a relative's health fails, all involved are often fearful of what the future holds: nervous of the pain and difficulties ahead. The family most in need of support may even find that other relatives distance themselves.

Isn't it true that when the need is greatest, support from our nearest and dearest is sometimes at an all-time low?

But it's not necessary to ring round after them for help, alienating others and frustrating yourself when they list their reasons why they *can't* help. Far more helpful would be to sit quietly and gather your thoughts; thus allowing guidance to come from your inner resources. This way the powers that be within all concerned can deal with the trauma calmly, rationally and objectively; thus making your own involvement that much easier.

Even when the time arrives that you've been dreading – the final departure of a loved one from this world – that, too, can be managed in peace and tranquillity. When your thoughts are aligned with your soul, you'll be more confident that all are being cared for.

ADDICTIONS

At every age and stage of life human beings regularly need a source of comfort or escape: something they can rely on to get them through the day.

A baby or toddler might suck his thumb, young girls lose themselves in the imaginary world of their dolls; teenagers spend hours on Facebook; and housebound mums often seek solace in daytime television.

Such distractions all bring a form of comfort and escape from the pressures of daily life.

However, before long the thumb-sucking child becomes a teenager. He hasn't outgrown the need of a comforter, yet cannot continue the childish habit; pride and rude comments from his friends won't allow it. But the deep-rooted insecurity behind his need of a comforter is still there.

As he grows up he enters the world of peer pressure and is expected to try what other guys and girls indulge in: souped-up cars, cigarettes, alcohol, drugs, sex and petty crime. Once the breaking-in period is over and he no longer chokes on the smokes or throws up after a six-pack, he realises these new comforters remove his inhibitions. He likes this and tries them more often. They're a good way to escape reality and nagging adults.

...A bit hard on the pocket, though.

Then he's introduced to drugs, which blow his mind and give him highs he never knew existed. Who needs worries now? Time passes and he is hooked. What happens next is a matter of record; desperately sad for all but the lucky few who escape the downward spiral.

A pattern has been set for life – or at least, for a long time to come.

Drugs, cigarettes and alcohol are hard to give up, not only because they are physically addictive, but also because they offer pleasure instead of pain and peace instead of turmoil. As long as the supply is regular, the user doesn't care too much about anything else.

Nevertheless, all 'good things' must come to an end. Sooner or later his addiction catches up with him. He's kicked out of school and home; watched by the police or a local gang; is always broke, and even steals to finance his next fix. Gradually he gets into the hard drugs that will lead to his undoing.

Whatever we get involved with, whether it's the worrying scenes of drugs, crime and gambling; or something more acceptable like social media and compulsive shopping, we can become so trapped that we sink deeper and deeper; cut off from normal living, and unable to climb out.

But what if somebody were to offer a natural way out, with little or no cold-turkey; with highs less dramatic but of a permanent nature and with few side effects; which didn't cost a cent and was in itself non habit-forming? Do you think an addict would be interested?

...Would *you* be interested?

The effects of over-eating can be as harmful as the effects of drug or alcohol abuse. Anyone with a weight problem knows how demoralising it is to keep piling it on. These days it is widely acknowledged that compulsive eating is not due to hunger, but to the desire for comfort foods. Eating to excess is an attempt to fulfil a need. The longing for fulfilment by taking something in through the mouth can be as strong as the sensation obtained when smoking a cigarette.

The desire for physical sensation, even that achieved by swallowing, is activated by a feeling of emptiness: not of the stomach, but of the soul.

This can manifest as indecision or stress, as loneliness or insecurity, and that ever-present sense of longing. Over-eaters tend to be women: mothers who are stuck at home with the children, teenagers with low self-esteem; people alone with no friends, partner or pet for company; others with no hobby or occupation to fill their day, and with little motivation to look for a stimulating or rewarding life.

What's not so widely acknowledged is this: When the emptiness is redressed, the desire to overeat lessens. With eating less comes loss of weight; with loss of weight comes a feeling of well-being, and with a feeling of well-being comes increased self-esteem, and the longed-for desire to get up and go.

Any eating disorder has its root cause. The insatiable desire to be slim, which can develop into an all-consuming habit, is born of a great need and sustained by addiction. It could be the result of problems in the home, from low self-esteem, or the compulsion to keep up with the fashion of skinny bodies. Again, the need is created within the soul's great void, and shows itself as an eating disorder.

Replenish the emptiness in the soul; cure the habit aspect of the disorder, and the eventual result is nothing short of miraculous.

Such cures from alcoholism, drug addiction and eating problems are not unknown. It isn't always necessary to go to a clinical therapist for treatment, although that is a proven option.

However, if the individuals concerned have had enough of institutions, clinics and fitness centres, and if they are able to recognise the tremendous force lying dormant in them, in time they could help to bring about their own cure.

They wouldn't need to break off their habit straight away; that would be trying to exercise willpower they may not yet have gained. But with perseverance and faith in their inner Self, they could gradually bring themselves to a stage where they no longer want to continue with these comforters.

Furthermore, the situations that undermined their self-esteem or drove them to seek external comforters in the first place, would begin to seem unimportant.

HOBBIES AND ENTERTAINMENT

There are approximately sixteen hours in the waking day. During this time we like to keep ourselves occupied: to be doing something to tax our minds and our bodies, and to earn a living.

The period of time we know as the working week is generally required for responsibilities to family, school or work. At the weekend we utilise our time in pursuits of a different kind: driving the children to a Saturday fixture, painting the house, supporting the Lions Club, and so on.

So throughout each week, plenty of work occupies our days, with time left over for leisure activities of our own choosing: to our pastimes.

The hours we devote to pastimes could be divided into two categories:

Firstly, there's the musician who's in his element when playing in front of an audience; the mountaineer who is at peace when pursuing his interest; and there's the devoted mother whose love for her children is so strong that she wants nothing more than to be with them.

Secondly, there's the beneficiary who is unable to hold onto a job and seeks the company of others for something to do; or the husband who spends much of his time at the tavern because he's miserable at home. And then there's the youth who is urged to take up a sport in order to 'get out of himself.'

The first type of person is complete in himself, and his or her interest merely enhances an already fulfilling life, whereas the second type is basically unfulfilled and seeks escape or comfort by way of his preferred pastime.

Even people who do valuable work in the community may fall into these categories. Some might be happy while working on a project, but sink into a meaningless rut when back at home.

When it comes to our pastimes, wouldn't the ideal be to enhance our free time rather than use it as an escape; to savour the icing on the cake instead of depending on the fruit cake itself? If we could wash away any deep-rooted problems or a sense of emptiness and bring ourselves to a plateau of fulfilment whereby we need no escape, then we'd enjoy our pastimes to the full.

That seeking and searching, wanting satisfaction, escape or excitement would be replaced by contentment with any enjoyment that does come our way. We would no longer need to look outside of ourselves for personal fulfilment, or to escape down the road to the pub.

And believe it or not, those committed hours of the week, however they are spent, would seem much less of a drudgery, and even pleasurable.

DAILY SUPPLY

The most astounding aspect of this energy within our souls is the tangible evidence of its existence. Most of the benefits we reap from it involve thoughts and emotions; but there is nothing invisible about some of the things that can happen. This is where the natural law of attraction; the law of need and supply, of cause and effect, is most noticeable – if we're alert enough to notice.

Beneficial things do happen for us all the while, only we don't recognise them. The rational aspect of our thinking stops us from acknowledging that we *are* being provided for – when things happen as a result of coincidence, out of the blue, or for no apparent reason.

We might have cause to say "I nearly had a nasty fall today," without considering, 'but I *didn't* fall.'

Or how about, "Last week my father-in-law almost died from a viral infection," yet fail to acknowledge that he's now much better.

We place the emphasis on 'I nearly got hurt,' whereas it ought to be on 'but I didn't.'

Can you see a pattern here? Is it coincidence, or is it that we're oblivious to a truth that's been around us all the time? Are we somehow reluctant to admit that in many instances all is well?

Yes, often we do lack a sense of gratitude, but only out of unawareness. After all, you can't say 'thank you' if you aren't aware you're receiving something.

Once we begin to recognise this, a new world opens up and we see how subtly our needs are being met.

Many things flow to us imperceptibly, and we barely notice. Maybe they've been part of our lives for so long that we now take them for granted.

Other things stand out a mile.

For example, I once had a large bill to pay and didn't know where the money would come from. When the bill came due I worked out how much I would have on hand to contribute to it, and to my utter amazement it was the exact amount. This incident was especially memorable for me because it was my first awareness of such activity. Prior to that, I would have put it down to coincidence. Now I notice it in many aspects of my life.

The flow of the life-force through everything is continuous. It provides for us in a material sense as well as humanly; even though we may not be aware of it, put it down to other influences, or attribute it to our own efforts.

Too often, we attribute success to our own efforts: the money we earn, the good health we enjoy, the skills we develop. Never does it occur to us that what we need is being supplied; or at least that we're given the means of attaining it.

Just as a hungry sparrow has to search for the worms he is to eat – they surely don't come looking for him – so do we have to search, to study or to work for our supply. But once we've opened ourselves up to the spirit and are continually aware of its activities; when we genuinely need something and reflect on it without worrying, we're more likely to receive whatever it is we need.

However, if we worry it might not happen, or are too specific as to what it should be, then it probably won't!

When we allow the life-force to flow through us it will provide for and protect us; not in such a manner that we're tempted to be greedy, but as and when we need it.

For instance, the effect of rising prices doesn't hurt as much: a blessing to anyone. The week's grocery purchases last a week, and not six days as in the past. No matter how little time there is, we fit in all that needs doing without stress. Invariably there's a parking space when we're looking for one. A family member gets hurt enough to learn a lesson, but not enough to cause serious injury. And so the list goes on, for it is part of the continuous flow of energy through our lives.

We like to decide for ourselves what we need. When it's not forthcoming we react alarmingly; even complaining that nothing ever happens as we want it to. Yet what we really need is not the same as what we *think* we need, and it's what we really need that's supplied.

Perhaps this is why we don't take too much notice of the positive occurrences in our lives; and instead of being appreciative, we're disappointed.

Our requirements are being supplied to us at this very minute, but you wouldn't think so when you read the tabloid papers, watch television and listen to the gloomy outlook for the planet. As a result, we spend a lot of time focusing on all the worries, and ignore the good things that also happen.

Bearing in mind the unblemished evolution of our species, there's not much chance our inner resources will leave us stranded. Life itself will not cease – and neither will it stop providing for us if we remain connected to it.

Haven't all the so-called human inventions throughout the ages really been discoveries that were made when needed; then put into a workable form? Think about the discovery of oil. When it was first noticed seeping from the ground, a means of using it was firstly invented and then brought into common use. Nowadays, alternative forms of energy are being developed.

The seeds of inspiration are planted in the scientist or inventor when the practical use of a commodity is needed, and eventually it becomes an invention.

They say, 'necessity is the *mother* of invention.'

Maybe that should read, 'necessity is the *inspiration behind* invention.'

PIECES IN A JIGSAW

When some insight into our problems has been gained, we're then in a position to step onto the ladder's next rung. In doing so, we may discover the meaning of life revealing itself through our own observations. Precious thoughts may come to mind to uplift the soul. Ordinary day-to-day life is viewed from a different perspective, and gradually our outlook on just about everything changes and becomes more positive.

This might seem impossible, almost laughable at the moment; yet give it time and you'll see for yourself.

Things like sayings, proverbs and quotations from books; lines from songs, poems and hymns: those familiar words we may not have given much thought to in the past, come to life and begin to take on meaning. The old feeling of wanting excitement or something to look forward to gradually wanes. We begin to take pleasure in what we have, be it ever so humble; to appreciate what is ours without wanting more. The things that once irritated don't seem so irksome, and if they do then all that's required is a moment or two in the inner sanctuary of the soul.

There, we quickly recharge our batteries and recover some composure.

We come to recognise that each of us is an individual, and no matter in what poor light we may once have regarded ourselves, we realise it was merely our poor minds at work and has nothing to do with the real identity deep within.

We are all individual and beautiful, and only became unhappy or resentful because our true nature was buried.

Each of us is like an iceberg: only the tip is visible. Only the nagging relative, the apathetic lout, the drunken old man are visible to the human eye. But the greater part of the iceberg cannot be seen from above the water level because we're looking at it darkly. No other part of each other is visible. Once life reveals itself, the 'water' clears and we're able to discern the hidden depths.

If only we could penetrate our own hidden depths and that of others too, wouldn't it be enlightening? We would be drawn so much closer to each other, knowing that deep down inside we're all much the same, with similar worries and aspirations.

We are just as important, just as 'normal' and just as talented in our individual fashion, even if that talent has not yet revealed itself.

We're like cogs in a wheel. Many cogs and wheels may make up the machine, yet if a single cog is broken the operation of the machine is disrupted.

We are as pieces in a jigsaw, where if only one piece is missing the puzzle is incomplete.

Each of us has a different role to play in life; not so much whether we're to be cab drivers or brain surgeons but rather our own part in the universal scheme of things; even if we may never consciously know what that part is to be.

The power in the universe expresses itself as the things of this world, and also through them. It appears as a sleek, unique bird, and through the bird as song.

It manifests as a human being – and through the human being as individual interest, talent and skill.

We don't all have the same interests, talents and skills. If we did, the world would not be well-balanced. As pieces in the jigsaw we are basically the same but with different, individual markings; together making up something of great diversity. Not all the jigsaw pieces are rich in colour, some are plain; but if all the pieces were bright and none were plain the resulting picture would lack interest.

It truly does take all sorts to make a world.

We are each marked with a different component of the universal picture, so why should we feel cheated or inadequate if our own markings are fairly plain? Even a completely blank piece still has part of the picture on it and helps to make up the whole.

I believe our purpose as human beings should be to discover the way in which we're each 'marked,' and how to develop it.

Our education systems generally push youngsters towards academic or professional careers. This is such a shame.

Every form of occupation is vital, whether in the field of brain surgery or driving that cab. Qualifications may be a necessary requirement in the job market these days, yet just because we're not academically brilliant it doesn't mean we don't excel in other ways. All forms of employment bring out individual skills, talents and merits, whether it's the amount of brainpower required or the ability to hold down a monotonous job.

What's more, the roles we play are of equal importance to the balance of the whole; not judging by our skills, but by the disruption if that particular service is withdrawn. We have all been affected when nurses, airport staff or members of the fire brigade go on strike. It provides the community with as worthwhile a service sweeping roads as it does playing at political leadership – and it's usually more appreciated, too.

People whose creative talents have surfaced and been allowed to develop are those who've broken free of the materialistic world. Having shaken off their age-old hang-ups they're now at peace with their environment and, more importantly, with themselves. Even though they still live as ordinary people they've also given themselves the freedom to develop their talents. They recognise that the gift to the world that's being demonstrated through them is as important as their everyday roles, and plays just as necessary a part.

If people like Chopin or Monet, Elvis Presley or Agatha Christie had said, "I can't be a composer, an artist, a singer or a writer today, because I must devote all my time to workplace and family," then the artistic world would be the poorer for it.

We all have a measure of talent. If at this moment you're thinking *you* don't have any talent, it's not that you have none; but rather that you haven't yet recognised your talent and allowed it to develop. There could still be that weight of pressure stopping the hidden depths from being revealed.

Once, when I was approaching a milestone birthday, I dreaded the prospect of its arrival because I had nothing to show for it.

My attitude was, "What have I accomplished in my life? I can't even bake a decent cake."

If somebody told me that one day I'd be 'sitting on top of the world', and writing about it, I would have laughed. I felt nothing but bitterness for life in general, and empty regarding myself. How then could I ever consider feeling good about life – let alone setting it down on paper? How can something positive *ever* come out of such negative thoughts?

The answer is: it can't.

While there is tension and turmoil in the mind, body and soul, there can be no peace or creativity. First, we should rid ourselves of the turmoil and substitute peace of mind, so that creativity has a chance to blossom. Then and only then will we begin to see wonders take place.

So, consider if you will, that in two months' time – or two years or even two decades – you might also be 'sitting on top of the world' and achieving something you or your family never thought you could.

This doesn't mean we're all going to be artists, composers, authors or singers. Not all of us can be brightly coloured pieces in the jigsaw. Talent shows itself in *many* different ways.

If everybody was good at painting there would be nobody left to just appreciate art. Being a lover of music, whether it's classical, jazz or rock, is as much a talent as being able to write it or play a musical instrument. Being a good listener is as much a talent as having a way with words. Anything we are good at is in itself a talent to one extent or another. Anything we genuinely enjoy doing, creating or achieving, whether it's making cupcakes or tinkering with old cars: that is talent; that is our gift to the world which could be allowed to develop.

It's not the degree of success in our chosen field that's important, but the fact that we are able to recognise our true identity and our underlying potential, and then go on to claim our role in life.

We are related one to another by a common thread of identity. Nobody is less or more vital than anyone else.

Whatever circumstance we blame for making us what we appear to be, it's really the human mind that over the years has reacted to outer conditions.

In effect, we become the person our minds direct us to become.

Once we've uncovered the nucleus of our being, the fortress walls gradually crumble, revealing us as we really are: a vital piece in the 'jigsaw' of life.

The remedy for every factor that enters our lives may be found – at least initially; at least in part – by focusing in meditation and drawing out from our souls whatever is needed through normal, everyday channels.

The basis for the answers to all of our problems could be obtained from this source, if given the chance. It comes to us not with a flourish, but subtly, naturally, almost imperceptibly; in a fashion that anyone else would call luck or coincidence. When we witness it at work in our lives time and time again, we start to recognise that it's not mere coincidence.

Our lives begin to lose their complicated aspect, and yet we know that of ourselves we have done nothing except open up and *allow* it to happen.

We might not be able to understand how it happens; it just does. We probably couldn't explain it to other people even if we wanted to, and certainly could provide no proof of our claims. It would be pointless to try, for this is one of life's mysteries.

From our earliest days we're taught that it's better to give than to receive; that we should spend more of our time at work than at play, and that where possible we must generally cultivate selflessness. These again are things we've been led to believe. Once we've acknowledged our inner identity, and learnt to respond to intuition instead of the insistence of others, we can put all this into a better perspective.

Gradually we come to recognise that we, too, are worthy of consideration; not selfishly ignoring the needs of those in our care, but giving ourselves a little respect, a little thought and a little time. We need some time to get to know ourselves better, even to like ourselves; time perhaps to reflect on the fundamentals of life, of which we are a part.

Time to develop the simple or glorious talents given to each of us as individuals, whatever form they may take. And even time to have a much needed rest.

To make ourselves stop rushing about, if only for a moment or two, and benefit from the inner calm and freedom that can be ours.

We're encouraged to 'shape up' and make something of ourselves; even to change for the better as though there's something wrong with us. This in itself is wrong. Imagine the workings of a new car: To begin with it's in mint condition and performing as it should. With the passage of time, if it's cared for and maintained regularly then it remains in good working condition. If it's neglected, abused and allowed to deteriorate, then it ceases to perform properly. Yet at any stage, it can go into the workshop, receive careful attention and be brought back to its intended state. There's no wrong to be righted, merely a condition to be improved upon.

...And the same applies with us.

We've done nothing wrong that we need to have righted. We've just neglected ourselves inwardly; to such an extent that we've lost sight of our intended state.

But we can bring ourselves back to that state if we've a mind to, by turning inwards and spending time in our own 'workshop'. There, the overhaul, although lengthy and not without difficulties, is both worthwhile and effective.

After all, we can only give of ourselves, whether of money, love, or health and strength, if we have something to give. When a car has broken down or is out of petrol, it won't go. If we're feeling empty inside, then before we can think about giving, first we must receive. Even a brand-new vehicle needs regular petrol and oil. When we've received rest, love, consideration or self-respect, one day we might actually *want* to give.

We shouldn't feel guilty about allowing ourselves some consideration. It's our right; we are worth far more than machines.

Life holds nothing but promise; its eternal existence, of which we are a part, is assured.

It is continuous, like electricity flowing around a circuit with no sense of time and space.

The obstacles in our way are experiences set in place as foundation stones of a richer awareness of life – not to be dwelt on or held against us.

There is nothing to fear from the flow that is life itself. Our protective instincts will lessen danger, accident and anxiety. If troubles come our way, we should get through them comparatively unruffled; for we will have left behind the stressful effects of worry, as a child outgrows his toys.

We've at long last moved up the ladder to something better and more rewarding – and nothing's going to stop us now.

THE PRICE TO PAY

The simplicity of this theory may seem incredible, but also unbelievable and I wouldn't blame a sceptic for thinking, "What a load of rubbish – I don't believe a word."

Yes, it's natural to give judgment on hearsay. Yet, if you're not prepared to try new things out for yourself how can you know your judgment is correct?

You may be told that white-water rafting is great fun, but you'll only find out for certain if you give it a try.

To obtain anything worthwhile in life we have to use our initiative; in this case by making the first move and applying some effort to get things going. That door to opportunity still needs to be opened. The same approach applies to the benefits we reap from our inner resources. We must work to obtain them. However, if we adopt a 'half full' attitude and don't give up at the first sign of adversity, it can be pleasant and rewarding.

I know how it feels to be stuck in the nightmare, but I also know what it's like to have awakened from it. The only price I had to pay for the benefits gained was to regularly seek connection with my inner resources. So I urge anyone down in the dumps to decide here and now to exit that social media site, get up from the couch and open the door of opportunity.

Once you've made the first move, you'll need to pluck up every ounce of courage and initiative you possess to set the wheels of progress in motion. Some will begin to notice the benefits straight away; for others it may take a while. It all depends on how much effort, or rather how much perseverance you are prepared to put in.

Attaining a constant liaison with this unseen life-force may be fraught with ups and downs, but the benefits are 'out of this world.' Any young boy knows the juiciest apples are at the top of the tree. If he's keen enough to get at them he doesn't mind the odd scratch on the way up.

This is a brand-new venture and will need appropriate groundwork.

When you're undertaking any adventurous new project, whether planning a landscape painting or putting up a fence, the job will require a fair amount of preparatory work. Such preparation involves time, effort and patience before the main work can begin. Yet you still do it because you know you're preparing the way for something that will ultimately net results.

To routinely focus your attention inwards is the only preparation required, and the only effort involved in this is to cultivate the art of patience. Dispelling some of the stress on a regular basis maintains the flow of awareness not into, but *out of* ourselves.

The emphasis is not so much on *doing,* as on *letting*; not a question of trying to make things happen, but rather allowing them to develop from within us.

You don't even need to physically withdraw from what you're doing. It's possible to contemplate while doing the ironing or working in the garden; it will still bring this outward flow of life and truth into operation.

With time and practice the flow becomes continuous; but if you lapse into old habits if only for a day or so you'll notice the difference. The pull of human conditioning is strong, and difficult to rise above once you've slipped back into it. So if you realise this new experience is for you, first of all don't be afraid to admit it to yourself. There's no need to tell others; they probably wouldn't understand. Then you must go all out to maintain it.

We're all 'only human' and susceptible to slipping back.

If you can, plan a regular vigil. This won't be such a hard thing to do once you get used to it. Some people use a vitamin supplement. A small amount is taken at regular intervals to keep a good balance health-wise. It would be no good ingesting a whole week's supply on a Monday and assuming the effect will last until the following Monday. Supplements don't work that way – and neither does the boost we get from our inner resources.

...Yes, little and often is the secret.

If you can keep it up, you've everything to gain. If you let it slip, it's a long haul up again. Turn your back on it and it lies dormant instead of remaining active.

Once a routine has been established, there's no hurry. It will be tempting to rush things, but that's just impatience creeping in. The ingrained habits of a lifetime cannot be changed overnight. If we're not prepared to be patient, then we lose out and sink back into the nightmare.

Remember, it's not a person doing the work, but rather the invisible energy within a person. We have no right to try and hurry it along.

It's like catching the bus to work. You get on it, pay your fare and sit down. When you arrive at your destination you get off. But do you give any thought to the actual journey? You've ascertained it's the correct bus and have found a seat. Then what do you do – read an ebook, talk to your neighbour, do a puzzle, look out of the window? There are many ways in which people can pass the time while riding on a bus. But do passengers ever wonder if it will break down or if the bus-driver is competent? Not usually. They just get on with what they normally do, knowing that the driver will take them safely to their destination. And that's how it should be with our spiritual journey.

Our inner resources can only be stimulated when we become aware of them, and focusing inwards eventually brings this about. But this is all we must do. It's all we *can* do. Nothing else is required except that when our intuition speaks, we'd be well-advised to listen and respond.

Don't be mistaken when it does speak, either: It may shout so loudly within your mind that it knocks you for six, or it may whisper quietly while you're thinking of something else and you fail to notice. Very often the right motivation is there, yet is so swamped by mind rambling that it can't get through.

Neither does it prompt you at a convenient time: You might be having a snooze on a Saturday afternoon when your conscience insists you get up and mow the lawns. You could be out binge drinking when you suddenly realise you've had enough. You're chatting on the phone to a friend and the thought pops into your head, "Don't forget to take the meat out of the freezer." Or, resentful towards your mother over something, you might find yourself needing to apologise even though you weren't at fault.

Such prompts can pop up spontaneously: Sometimes they take you by surprise, and tell you to do things you don't want to do. It may take all your effort to respond: to mow the lawn or put down the drink. But make that first move, however reluctantly, and you'll feel better for it in the long run.

However when the promptings are ignored, things will often go wrong: You can't even be bothered getting the mower out of the shed, and it rains for a week; you ignore the nudge to reconcile with your mother, and remain at loggerheads for the rest of the year; you tell yourself, "I'll do *that* job later," and finish up by forgetting it altogether.

These inner promptings relate to all aspects of our lives. Over the years we learn how to respond to even the most subtle of them, trusting we're being shown the right path to follow.

So relax, cultivate patience and listen closely to your intuition. That's not too big a price to pay for the freedom of life itself, is it?

Listen to your intuition instead of that rambling mind, which has been your undoing. Listen to your intuition instead of to popular opinion, which may let you down. Listen to your intuition; don't ignore your problems – *that*, you already know, doesn't solve anything.

Listen to your intuition; it's the only thing that takes care of your best interests.

Wake up from the nightmare you've previously thought of as Life. Take courage in both hands, live and be free.

You have all the backing you need.

PART TWO

CHANNELLING THE SPIRIT

To discover, recognise and activate our own intuition is one of life's saving graces. It appears to the individual as a gift, while at the same time it's a natural right: a heritage of sorts. Except, it's not part of our human heritage – that wearisome baggage that we've been carrying around – so much as a spiritual birthright.

Many people are intuitive, or spiritually awakened, but with no conscious awareness of such. It has always been part of their makeup and is therefore normal to them.
  You'll find these inspired people everywhere, and even know some of them by name.
  There's the man in the corner shop who always has a smile no matter what the weather, the youngster who is naturally kind and loving, the scruffy old woman down the road who writes deeply moving poetry; or maybe even the handicapped young girl who plays the piano exquisitely.
  In the main, the spiritually-awakened are very ordinary to look at. They don't wear distinctive clothes or even live in communes. Basically, they're just regular people who live in city suburbs or out in the country, and make ends meet like the rest of us. Where they differ is that they're generally more at peace within themselves. They have opened up the channel to the intuitive, spiritual side of their identity, whether or not they're aware of it.

However, becoming aware of your spiritual identity is a definite advantage. It means you can tune in at any time to receive inspiration. It will provide you with a sense of comfort or strength when faced with unexpected hurdles.

Within you has been created a central core that, with time and practice, can become resilient against forces that might adversely affect you.

As the spirit within is increasingly activated so, too, is the phenomenon of spiritual grace. It is given to us in direct proportion to the amount of attention we pay to it.

Just as a baby suckling at its mother's breast stimulates the flow of milk, and the more it suckles the greater becomes the flow, so it is with our spirituality. The more attentive we are to it, the more we benefit from it. Our inner batteries are recharged every time we plug into the power source; not unlike recharging the battery from a cellphone or similar gadget.

But if the baby decides it doesn't want to suckle any more or the user of the phone forgets to recharge it, then the supply dries up.

Acknowledging your spiritual identity is another step up the ladder. From your fresh vantage point you can look down at the closeted life you've left behind, and see reality in a brand new light.

When you were still on the bottom rung of the ladder everything would have seemed dull, lifeless and lacking colour. The 'colours' in life were there; but weren't an intrinsic part of your experience. Now, as you recognise unseen aspects of your life, you become aware of all the colours.

Looking at it another way: If the reception on your old analogue television was so bad that you could only get a clear picture on one channel, you might not have even considered that there could be other, better channels on offer. However, once you make the switch to digital and as a result gain all its benefits, you are relieved to have moved on from analogue.

When you're stuck in a dreary rut you cannot know there is a spiritual side to your life that far surpasses what you're presently experiencing, unless you make the switch.

The intrinsic nature of mankind *is* actually spiritual. That mystical facet of our being, although intangible, is the real driving force behind our lives. However, there's another aspect of this driving force to be considered apart from our own part in it, and that is the source of the energy itself.

If you're thinking there's something vaguely familiar about all of this only under a different guise, then you're on the right track. Up until now we've thought in terms of our 'inner resources' – the spiritual centre of our being. Yet, there is another way of looking at this great mystery:

Imagine the concept of humanity's inner or spiritual nature and our exterior, worldly nature as the shape of a wheel. Or more precisely: a cart or bicycle wheel, where the outer rim and the hub are connected by spokes. For our analogy, the wheel is lying flat on the ground.

Please take a moment to picture this.

The rim of the wheel equates with the outer aspect of our nature, and the hub of the wheel to the centre of our being.

In this comparison, we live our worldly lives around the rim, whereas the energy that drives us is at its centre. The two are connected by a spiritual 'channel'; or in this instance, the spokes of the wheel.

Now we'll look at it from a different perspective: Imagine the wheel as a three-dimensional object, by drawing up its centre into the shape of a cone; or better still, the conical form of a mountain.

Viewing it side on, that which we first regarded as the wheel's hub has been elevated to the *top* of the mountain, and the rim of the wheel is now around the *base* of the mountain. Could this be the concept that seems familiar?

We stand at the bottom of this hypothetical mountain and gaze up its great height to the summit. A climb to the top seems unthinkable, therefore we don't try. No one but the most enterprising of mountaineers would attempt such an ascent of a physical mountain, and climbing up to spiritual heights is the same.

So the majority of us remain at its base, separated from the peak by what seems like an insurmountable distance.

Can you see what has happened to our simple wheel hub: the centre of our being? It has turned into a distant mountain peak: separate and insurmountable.

The mountain peak as stated here should equate with the hub of the wheel, should it not? Yet it appears to have become something completely different and separate; so it can't be the same – and yet it is.

...How perplexing.

What then is at the top of the mountain if it's no longer the centre of our being? The answer is this:

The summit of the mountain is indeed still the same as the hub of the wheel, albeit viewed from a different angle.

Many of us have grown up believing in something greater than ourselves, which we consider to be high above us. Some great and powerful wisdom, so we've been taught, created the universe and oversees its handiwork. Of this fact the majority of us seem to be in agreement. We have even given it an imaginary form: a bearded old man sitting up on a cloud gazing down upon humanity, or maybe perched on the top of a mountain. Sometimes we think of it as compassionate, sometimes we see it as omnipotent, but always it's 'above' us and separate from us.

...And what am I talking about?
(Surely you've guessed by now!)
I refer, of course, to God.

The hub of the wheel, that wonderful, beautiful centre of our being – accessible to all who open up to it – is exactly the same as the deity at the top of the mountain: the mysterious, unseen God from whom we ordinary folk have experienced a sense of separation since time immemorial.

Isn't it true that in many Western countries we have distanced ourselves from God?

Isn't it also true that a great many of us have no real idea about the entity referred to as 'God;' that even the mention of the word sends some of us running for cover, because either we feel unworthy of Him or we're isolated from something that we deem alien to our existence?

Herein lies the greatest quandary of the last millennium – and the reason why so many of us feel as though we're immersed in a nightmare.

A SEPARATE STATE

Many people throughout the world, today and in times gone by, have considered that as there is such order in the universe some kind of wisdom or force must be behind it.

To that force our ancestors gave the name 'God.'

Yet, although our entire spiritual universe is contained within the human soul, down through the ages successive generations created an illusion of separation between us and that universal God. As a result, we've come to think of our Creator as being in control of the universe from 'up there,' and have got into the habit of praying to Him to come *down* and help us.

We are aware of the workings of nature on the face of this planet, and openly proclaim how wonderful it is. Even so, somehow we've overlooked the fact that the power behind the universe and the power behind nature are one and the same thing.

Furthermore it would never occur to some that we, as human beings, have anything to do with either; as though we are a separate entity both from the universe and from nature.

What an illogical way of thinking!

We are the rim connected to the centre of the wheel; the base attached to the summit of the mountain. We're a drop in the ocean of the universe, so how can we be anything but part of it?

And as individuals we are all vital pieces in the universal jigsaw puzzle.

For centuries, Western civilisation has searched upwards for the Creator instead of inwards, thereby erroneously establishing itself as something separate from God. Yet in essence we are a living manifestation of God; the power of the universe joyfully expressing itself as and through the life-forms we call human beings. It is the collective minds of both current and previous generations that created the separation.

Poor misguided humanity. No wonder we can't escape from that wretched fortress.

Needless to say, the presence or energy that we refer to as God is 'out there' as well. There would be no universe at all if it – or He – was *not* out there (and for convenience I shall refer to God as 'He').

However, where the spiritual needs of each person are concerned – whether in the streets of New York City or the backblocks of Australasia – God, the universal spirit; our guiding, sustaining life-force, lies within the consciousness of each individual soul.

This is not the awareness of the rambling mind: the ego. It is a presence within the soul, which is experienced as a deep, inner conviction. Many of us do feel the peace and presence of God in our lives, but because of this inherited sense of separation we don't realise it's seated within us. We reach outside of ourselves, upwards to the distant peak, in order to touch and hopefully hold on to what we assume is there. But due to the illusory distance and sense of separation, we sometimes feel forsaken when we can't seem to grasp it.

Before my own awakening from the nightmare, I was certainly aware of God's presence in the universe and in nature. Yet although He was the God of everything else, I felt sure He had nothing to do with me. As far as I was concerned, I belonged within my fortress and God was either unable or unwilling to breach its walls. Yet the real problem lay not with God but with me, for I had lost the awareness of something that was intrinsically with me all along.

The lesson I learnt from this is that the external God will not connect with us if the door to the internal God is closed. He cannot help us if we don't first of all seek Him in the right place.

You may be inclined to say, "But I didn't know God was within my soul – or even that I had a spirit."

Perhaps you truly didn't know. As things stand, it's not surprising so many people don't know. The sense of separation is yet another piece of our inherited baggage. Unfortunately though, not knowing is barely a legitimate excuse; that is, a spiritually legitimate excuse. Even in everyday life, ignorance of a law is not acceptable.

Does the ocean let the sailor off for not knowing he should follow certain rules?

The same applies here. God, the energy source of the whole universe, won't accept anything but respect for His law either. We might not have known what the rules are, but we still have to suffer all the consequences for not following them.

The only real law; the most natural law in existence – the only price we have to pay for everything God has to offer – is that we comply with the rules and connect with Him absolutely. We don't need to ask for anything else. He already knows every one of our needs, for we've cried out about them frequently.

It is said that 'God is a jealous God.' If that's the case, then He has every right to be jealous; in fact aggrieved by our worship of worldly things. And sad, too, that humanity has created the sense of separation.

We have exiled God to the top of a very high mountain instead of embracing Him within the human soul.

It's still God's universe – not ours as we seem to think. He won't help us if we neglect Him, seek elsewhere for fulfilment or try to go it alone.

Is it any surprise that half the plans we make never turn out right? We are going about them entirely the wrong way. We're suffering the consequences for neglecting the natural laws of life; for not bothering to recharge our spiritual batteries.

Nevertheless, the Creator of our universe also knows that we're not entirely to blame for the separation, that we're not neglecting the laws wilfully. He knows our handed-down sense of separation and ignorance of His laws, together with the baggage we carry, made us consent to the situation. And when we do eventually hand control back to Him, all that's gone before is forgiven.

Even though we sometimes think otherwise, God has tremendous concern for us as individuals.

Don't forget, the energy that creates the galaxies can also help a newborn lamb to its feet. In asking us to make just one gesture – to seek Him and hand over the reins – He's giving us another chance to reconnect with His laws of life.

It's not as though we have to do anything, except to meditate. And when we begin to see this working, trust in the unseen develops naturally because we start to accept that it will not let us down.

People all through the ages have proclaimed the future of the world to be in the hands of our leaders or the military. Others have insisted it's to be found within a democracy or a stable community. Some even believe it is solely the responsibility of the family unit. But actually, the future of our planet and our race depends on what goes on inside the mind and soul of each individual person who is alive today.

It really is up to us; for as time goes by, if we don't develop the trust, offer that allegiance and adhere to the simple rules set down, then warmongering will continue and millions die in pandemics. Disasters will forever ravage the planet and its natural balance will remain in jeopardy. There will always be disharmony in our governments, our communities, our homes – and in our minds.

However, if everybody were to veer away from worldly thinking, and tuned in to the energy source within them, gradually the consciousness of mankind would be raised. Then the freedom and security of this planet will at last be restored, and there really could be 'peace on earth and goodwill towards men.'

This all sounds idealistic, I know; but when you come to think of it, what other solution is there? We've tried everything else and nothing is effective. Many times over we've attempted to gain lasting peace, to no avail.

Surely by now we've had enough of failure!

At present we're immersed in the politics of our respective nations: the 'system,' if you like. In a spiritual sense we can withdraw from the effects of this without causing mayhem. To withdraw to a vacuum would create isolation in our fortresses. To withdraw to the centre of our own souls is to find the guidance, peace and freedom to take us through the system we've hitherto known as 'Life'; not only on a personal or national level but also universally.

It's a question of dependencies. We're used to depending on others for just and fair treatment, by means of family, government, community and so on.
...But are they really dependable?
History has demonstrated that any achievement made through human effort is capable of crumbling. The fall of the Roman Empire and the demise of the Third Reich are examples of this. ...Why is that? Could it be because their dependencies were only on a human level?
They were established on foundations of sand rather than stone, and were doomed to fragment or disperse.

Think about the state of your world as it is right now. Is there universal peace, or even domestic harmony? Are all of the institutions and people around you living up to your expectations? Or are there flaws; is there corruption? Do you see dissension, deceit and human error? Have they made you feel free or insecure? It's your future that's in the hands of these institutions and individuals; your future and those of your children that are in jeopardy.
Now reflect upon the natural history of our world. Remove people from the scene and return to the hilltop overlooking the countryside; to witness again the gentle unfolding of nature. Reflect on all that you've read in the preceding pages here, and decide what you can really trust.
In effect, we've been placing our dependencies on the wrong source.

The road to real achievement and stability is via our spiritual resources – God: the only entity with the means of successfully evolving every aspect of human life.

You might be thinking, "That could be true, but I'm too stuck in my ways and too long in the tooth for changes now." However, when you're seeking freedom or security, it's never too late to open up a fresh page and start again. There's always some problem or a bad habit that has us in its grip, so ages or stages are never a barrier to success.

A question often asked is this: What is God?

What exactly comprises the presence that we call God? With which elements would this infinite source of energy be made up? And if you could actually see it, what form would it take?"

The usual answer is that God takes on the form of spirit, but how satisfactory an answer is that?

Does it give a clear indication of what He really is?

I don't doubt that if it were possible to put a finger on the exact identity of God there would be considerably more optimism in the world, and much less uncertainty. In fact, I don't believe there is a definite answer to that question. However, we *can* set our imagination to work and draw up a comparison.

From the roof of many a dance hall is found suspended an object known as a mirror-ball. This is a large revolving orb, the surface of which is covered with dozens of tiny mirrors.

A beam of light shines onto the orb, and as it reflects off the mirrors, flashes of light dance around the room.

Now put your imagination to work, and if possible, relate the mirror-ball to that which is God.

The Creator of the universe can be likened to the beam of light as it strikes the mirrors. When they 'flash' with light a baby is born, or a rose brought into being. A magnificent sunset may be formed or a beautiful melody created. A loving thought is transmitted, a new talent realised or an alternative source of power discovered. And then, even though it seems like many years or millennia, the light moves on.

The life-force thus takes on form. The infinite number of flashes coming off the mirror ball equals the number of ways in which it manifests as tangible being. Yet, as far as human beings are concerned, God 'flashes' within the body, mind and soul of all people; past, present and no doubt future, whether or not we're aware of it.

Westerners tend to regard things spiritual as belonging to another realm, but this is not so. It is with us in the here and now – in whatever we do and wherever we go. We can recognise it in feelings that 'warm the cockles of the heart.' The word 'spirituality' refers to those intense and inexplicable stirrings we may experience from this source, which is soul.

Soul isn't a part of the body, it's a state of being. Some might even say it's a vehicle for the spirit.

In the same way that the wheel's rim is connected to its centre by the spokes, so too is the soul connected with its spiritual centre; not separate from it but a vital part of the whole.

We think of the heavenly world as being 'out there,' beyond our sight and our senses. It isn't *only* out there, though. For sure, it may be in a galaxy far, far away, but it's also in the palm of a baby's hand and the smile of a mother.

It is invisible and intangible. It's as beautiful as a flower in bloom, striking as an ancient mountain range, dynamic as a symphony and as tender as a love affair. We are all part of it, and it is part of us.

Only the human mind has caused the separation from God, not God Himself.

Everything that exists now is as much a part of God as all that has gone before. Yet as far as the pattern of our own lives is concerned, it's what goes on deep within us that counts. And this aspect of our identity is just as important in the universal scheme of things – whatever that may be – as the flash that evolves into a new galaxy.

God 'flashes' in the universe as people and through people; as His creations and through His creations.

An ocean isn't only water; it's the water plus everything that the water contains. God is the whole universe plus everything in the universe, both seen and unseen; and that includes us.

I don't suppose anyone alive today knows all there is to know about God. But that doesn't stop us from feeling the presence deep within our souls, receiving inspiration and guidance throughout the course of our lives, and generally developing a close relationship with our Maker.

VARIATIONS ON A THEME

So far, all that's been written may provide something of an explanation, but it could also have opened up a 'Pandora's Box' of questions.

You'd be forgiven for thinking, "Yes, this is familiar, but not what I've heard before;" and this is right. Essentially it *is* different, yet at the same time recognisable; for you will have heard it stated in a different context, from another perspective and using strange terminology.

Whatever our race or culture, most of us are familiar with one or another of the world's great religions. The majority of these religions are based on worship of the one invisible God, but there any similarity ends.

Those who live in a predominantly Christian society are brought up with words like God, Heaven, Holy Ghost; sacred, divine, eternal and so on. These words are usually accepted by the believer or rejected by the sceptic. We may even have a limited, basic knowledge of the Old and New Testaments of the Bible, half-remembering stories we heard as children. Or we might never have gone to church, but are still familiar with church jargon.

Yet these are just words, and words are little more than a collection of letters until the reader of the words places an interpretation on them.

In the case of the word 'God,' one person may see Him as the bearded old man way up in the sky; another as the mastermind of the universe. Someone else may only think of Him in relation to what takes place inside a church.

We interpret all these words differently; often without fully understanding their true meaning.

To complicate matters further, an aspect of religion may be referred to by different names.

For instance, some of us can better relate to words like intelligence or spirit; to consciousness, wisdom and light, rather than God. And then there's the word 'church.' We all know what a church is – a place of worship. Yet there are many other words also used to describe our places of worship, such as temple, synagogue, chapel and mosque.

With these factors in mind, it's easy to see that there can be many interpretations and many words used to speak of the beliefs involved with the world's religions.

As with everything else, many traditions associated with the main religions were handed down from generation to generation, with a bit added here, something else altered there; human beings applying whatever doctrines were considered appropriate for their times.

In Victorian England, a Christian concept was that you were condemned to 'hellfire and damnation' if you chose not to attend church. I suspect they couldn't bear to see empty pews and collection plates; yet this demonstrates how humanity likes to complicate its religions. Nowadays, people seem to be more committed in their acceptance or rejection of religion. Yet the influences passed down from previous generations are still there, and the question of what religion is really all about still remains unanswered. This, so extensively, that the very idea of religion causes many people to cringe, because in this day and age it has become irrelevant to them.

Perhaps, then, it's time to look behind all of our inherited beliefs, and go back to Square One.
There is a piece of classical music called 'Rachmaninov's Eighteenth Variation on a Theme by Paganini.'
Quite a mouthful, you might be thinking. What does it have to do with religion?
It's true the music itself has nothing to do with religion, but take a closer look at the title:
Eighteen variations...on an original theme.
In this analogy, the religions which are based on the one invisible God, together with all their numerous sects and denominations, are the variations.
So what is the original theme?
...The God of all creation dwells within the soul of Man.

There doesn't seem to be very much similarity between the religions we have grown up with and the earlier part of this book, but in fact they relate to the same thing.
When I was young, we used to play a party game called 'Whispering.' A few of the guests stood in a row and the first person whispered a phrase or sentence to the next, who repeated what they thought they heard – in other words, their interpretation of what was said – to the third person, and so on down the line. By the time it came to the last person, who spoke it out loud, the statement no longer resembled the original sentence.
This is what appears to have happened through the centuries with our many perceptions of religion. Differing interpretations made by successive generations have been passed on to their descendants as absolute truth.

Historians claim the original truth behind the message of Jesus only lasted until about the third century, when variations began to be introduced. Since then they've been 'complicated' time and time again, right up to the present day, when in some respects they no longer resemble the original, simple message that was taught by Jesus himself.

If this is the case, then it's no wonder we're so mystified by all the variations.

Individual people see things very differently, one from the other. Imagine you're lecturing a class of students made up of an artist, a gardener, an aromatherapist, a secondary school teacher and a botanist. You hold up a single rose and ask them to jot down a brief description. Everyone describes it according to their perspective, and what they know about roses. No two definitions are identical, and yet all describe the same thing: a rose. An onlooker, anxious to be enlightened by the exercise, would be totally confused.

Aren't our inherited concepts about God and religion equally confusing? The eighteen variations on an original theme; the different descriptions of a single rose?

A billion people all over the world might have a billion different perspectives regarding the truth about God and religion.

The descriptions – the many variations of truth – are in the ancient and modern traditions adhered to, the diverse interpretations of scriptural principles; the perspectives adopted and the terminology used, whatever the origin of the sacred writings. Yet all relate to the same basic and often forgotten truth – that God, the guiding light for the universe, also dwells within the human soul.

This fact is as constant as the one which states that two-plus-two equals four, and that day will always follow night.

Only in the variations do we encounter complication and confusion.

...And the complications continue.

In the Seventies, a hippie song informed us we were at the dawning of the Age of Aquarius, which heralded yet another 'New Age' variation on our original theme. And now, in this third millennium since the time of Jesus, evangelical movements are aiming to popularise their own perspective. These give us yet more confusing standpoints to grapple with – or ignore, as the case may be. When will it all end?

Let's go back to the original theme and its simplicity.

Religion is the means by which we can attain the original theme in an ordered and disciplined manner, if we choose to. So often, though, religious perspectives place God on the high mountain rather than in the human soul.

Seeking God within ourselves is simplicity itself; yet scaling great and challenging heights to reach an elusive deity is an eternal struggle, and in recent times few have bothered.

Nevertheless, whatever journey of faith we do choose as we climb the ladder towards awareness, the spiritual aspect remains the same:

Our journey begins with basic humanity.

The destination is union with the source of life; which is the God within our universe and within our souls.

OUT OF DARKNESS

Somewhere at the beginning of time, when the Creator surveyed His universe and saw that it was good, there also came into existence another spirit; one which didn't quite fit the mould. This spirit went on, throughout the eons of time since then, to wreak as much havoc as it could; both in the world and within the minds of people. To this spirit we have also given a name: the devil.

Along with all things spiritual and religious, interpretation of this side of religion has been mostly left to speculation, as nobody was actually around to witness the event. But there is a story – some might call it a fable – which tells of how, at the beginning of creation, one of the angels in Heaven lost favour with God and was cast out. This angel's name was Lucifer. At the moment of Lucifer's expulsion there appeared a different face in the universe – one of darkness instead of light; an influence with which we associate words like evil, together with 'the devil,' Satan, demonic, hell, sinister and even something as relatively mild as 'negative.' And it would seem that whatever form it now takes, Lucifer has not gone away.

If the devil really is alive and well and still living on Planet Earth, then it's easy to understand why the world of today can seem so negative. Without the inner strength we gain from a firm connection with God, the forces of evil have the freedom to move where they will and invade whomever they choose.

And we, as mere mortals, are powerless to stop them.

Think of the negative influences at work in your own life right now; that confine you to your fortress and steel your liberty. Remember the nightmare in which it traps you, and out of which it prevents you from awakening.

Consider the problems, addictions or phobias that may have plagued you, and that seem impossible to overcome; the relationships that are regularly undermined by some sort of negative influence. Think of worldwide unrest and corruption, all of which appears at times to be controlled by something sinister; and even the soul-destroying belief that God has deserted you.

These are the work of the devil, and manifest as things 'going wrong' in our lives, both individually and globally.

Every time you ponder something negative; whenever you feel your spirits dropping, or react badly to a situation that displeases you; every display of arrogance and malicious intent; when you harbour anger and despair, or can't seem to resist a bit of temptation – on occasions like these you are opening up to negative influences.

These lapses unwittingly allow the devil to sneak in and wreak havoc in *your* mind and in *your* life.

There is a saying that puts it succinctly. It reads: 'When you turn your back on the light, you embrace the darkness and everything that lurks in it.'

The varying degrees of negativity attack us through our worldly thoughts and desires: the mental chains that bind; the aspects of our existence that keep us trapped in the nightmare. The devil is remorseless in its hold, and to free ourselves from its clutches is essential for healthy living as human and spiritual beings.

Think of the expressions used regularly that mention or involve the devil: 'give the devil his dues,' 'what the devil's got into you?' 'the devil finds work for idle hands,' 'the devil take the hindmost,' and 'what the hell do you think you're doing?' We employ them freely without thinking where they come from.

And there are other expressions that imply the invasion of a negative influence, such as, 'tempting providence' or 'making trouble for yourself.'

Think of the word 'pandemonium.' We all experience this at times: for instance, when guests at a party run riot or when things seem to go berserk. But have you ever thought what 'pandemonium' actually means? Look it up, and the dictionary will say something like, 'assemblage of demons.'

These expressions are not new. They have their origins in something pertaining to the devil and the negative side of life, and they relate to negative goings on in our lives even now; whether or not we believe in that sort of thing.

And when we do 'tempt providence' and invite these influences into our lives albeit unwittingly, it's 'the devil's own job' to kick them out again.

When the devil takes hold of the soul, the individual can be dragged down to the lowest depths of despondency.

Think of those said to be 'possessed' of evil spirits, with suicidal tendencies, a deep and abiding depression, or with some kind of condition that can't be identified. Blackness within the soul is irresistible to these negative forces, and the hapless victim doesn't stand a chance of recovering without something approaching a miracle.

Even on a superficial level, it takes a spiritually strong person to resist the temptations of the devil. These could be temptations which appear desirable or even good, but which are in fact a camouflage for something sinister – as in the expression, 'all that glitters is not gold.'

You can't see the devil any more than you can see God; but you can feel its influence in your emotions; you can witness its presence in your everyday life, and you already suffer along with the rest of humanity when it seems to be winning the battle between good and evil in our world.

...Except, the devil is not really winning; it just appears that way in the nightmare.

The individual who is spiritually asleep still experiences the full effect of negative forces. Yet the person who has awoken to the truth and recognises his relationship with God, develops the ability to rise above them. With time he learns how to avoid the devil's clutches.

This encourages a positive trend not only in his own life, but also that of anyone who comes close to him.

The devil need not be a problem once we've identified and then isolated the traits associated with it; when we have taken control by linking up with the source of our being, thereby restricting evil's access. We come under the protection of the Godhead, and only lose that protection when we relax our vigil, thus allowing the devil to drag us down again.

Yet even if that were to happen, by uttering the familiar words, 'Get thee behind me Satan,' as we link up with God again, the help and protection is there once more.

The promise of 'hellfire and damnation' may have been preached to the Victorians as a ploy to get them to go to church, but it is also a warning; an attempt to persuade the people to turn back to God. To prevent not only their own downfall but also that of the world: the Armageddon of ancient prophecy.

This is avoidable, but only if humanity functions as one great spiritual body; if we 'rise above' the devil's influence, and once more turn back to God.

The devil has done such a good job of wreaking havoc in our world that it sometimes makes me wonder if the angel called Lucifer was intentionally planted among us in order to make us suffer.

After all, it's through individual suffering that we learn, by learning that we grow spiritually; and *only* in that growing will we ascend the ladder to God.

Yes, indeed; it does make me wonder…

A POINT OF NO RETURN

A question arising from the above is this: If human beings are still a part of God, just how did this sense of separation first come about?

Why, instead of recognising Him at our centre, did we distance Him at the summit of an imaginary mountain, and then plummet into the waiting arms of Satan at its base?

Exactly when and how did we lose track of our spiritual heritage?

Our separation from God came about in the early days of human history: that is, in the early days of homo sapiens as a wise and spiritual entity.

Most of us will have heard the Bible story of Adam and Eve. In this story a serpent, alias the devil, tempted Eve with an apple from the forbidden Tree of Knowledge; then Eve tempted Adam who naïvely took a bite. This act of disobedience angered God; to the extent that He exiled them from the Garden of Eden, ever to restlessly roam the planet. After that time, with eyes focused on worldly attractions, future humans were lured even further away from God by the wiles of the devil.

Whether or not this actually happened nobody will ever know. Yet, as far as we today are concerned, it's symbolic of what's referred to as 'the Fall of Man;' when according to scripture we fell from God's grace and took on the burden of 'original sin.'

Throughout the ages that followed, modern man went his own way and developed a mind-set of independence from his source. Gradually he descended to the base of our spiritual mountain. There he found himself at a point of no return and surrounded by a negative environment. His children and his children's children came into being with scant knowledge of their intrinsic spiritual identity. Humankind, during the ages that followed, became selfish, worldly and isolated.

The rest of the story can be found in the Bible, some history books and on relevant websites.

As time advanced, the human individual began to realise that he wasn't doing as well as his earliest ancestors, and decided he should look for help. He recognised in his environment the influence of evil and didn't like what he saw. So he gazed up as though to the mountain peaks, seeking the great deity that actually formed the basis of his soul: a detail he was unable to remember.

In utter despair he cried out to God to come down and save him, for he didn't know how to scale it unaided. And when there was no satisfactory response he sank down into a pit of despondency; his empty soul trapped in a nightmare, his mind withdrawn into the fortress.

The sense of separation was complete.

Yet, despite mankind's ongoing sense of isolation he is still spiritually a part of God. It's only his perception of the situation that keeps him separate. He is now and always will be a drop in the ocean of God, even if that's a concept he's unable to grasp.

A drop of water becomes detached from the ocean and evaporates as it goes through its various transformations.

We experience it in the form of cloud, rain, ice, snow, lake and river, yet know that sooner or later it will return to the ocean. In such a way, we also return to God.

If only modern man had not fallen from grace. Think of all the pain and suffering he caused by being attracted to the devil's allure and renouncing his own soul.

Yet, the 'ocean' is still there; always ready and willing to receive each returning drop of water. The spiritual centre of every human being is never dead, but merely dormant; patiently waiting to be reawakened.

If each soul recognises that, as a drop in the ocean he is still a part of the whole, then he can break free from the negative influences that have governed his life. He will then be given the strength and guidance he needs in order to journey back to the source. As things stand though, it's likely to take a while; so great is the perceived distance between man and his God.

...It is still a very high mountain.

So, not only is the human soul making the arduous journey home, but also his progress is hindered by the fact that he has no conscious knowledge of such. This is why people feel lost, despondent and 'what's the point in it all?' in their attitude towards life. In a spiritual sense, they don't understand what's going on.

It's for this reason that we are drawn to the comforters in life; especially to drink and drugs.

When a person is under their influence they become 'high'. With minds lost in a temporary state of detachment they experience a false sense of soul. The high is achieved when the soul is artificially lifted within the human frame: above all the stresses that drive people to seek out such comforters. While the soul is elevated it feels very much at home: safe and secure in a strangely familiar environment. Ordinary life suddenly seems unreal and unimportant. The human effort needed, for example, to drive safely belongs temporarily to another world. Something like physical pain goes unnoticed.

Really, it's no wonder so many of us are attracted to drugs. We're unhappy souls trying to reach the summit of that mountain.

Nevertheless, the effect of the comforter soon wears off, and the 'low' experienced afterwards can be more devastating than the natural state beforehand. The soul longs to be elevated once again. Then, responding to the devil's taunts, the person reaches for another fix.

What few seem to realise is that this higher state will eventually be reached naturally, without need of artificial aids. It is attained free of effort or cost by experiencing the presence of God.

Due to our sense of separation, this elevated state is likely to be a gradual process: a steep and difficult ascent. Yet, where the soul of the person has awakened; when the distant summit has also been recognised as the hub of our being – when the true meaning of the 'colourful but empty splurge' in life's abstract painting has been revealed – then this whole lengthy process is more easily achieved.

At the moment Adam and Eve fell from grace, could they have considered that their actions might impose future hardship on the human race?

...It's doubtful.

If they'd realised the innocuous serpent was a really little devil, would they each have thought it through more carefully before taking the apple?

I wouldn't think so. After all, they were human, naïve, and susceptible to making mistakes.

Yet even now it's not too late for us to make amends and get back on track.

You see, when humanity falls so low that he's unable to pull himself up by his own bootstraps, God has a habit of helping out. One instance of this in particular was of very real significance.

A SECOND CHANCE

When mankind realised that he'd lost his way, God in His mercy must have decided that His progeny deserved a second chance, and went on to do something about it.

He somehow recognised that we humans had become too stubborn to learn the truth for ourselves, and that we needed something of a boost – an injection of His own consciousness – to demonstrate how we could reawaken to our spiritual reality.

This, apparently, could only be accomplished through the consciousness of another, very special human being.

So, when the timing was right, it was made known through the prophets of old that God would send us a spiritually enlightened person; someone with the authority to bring a message of hope to the whole world. Then, with luck and good management, humankind might listen.

This person became known as the 'Messiah.'

For centuries the coming of this saviour of mankind was foretold, though nobody truly expected it to happen in their own time. And when a baby was unobtrusively born in the Judean town of Bethlehem something over two thousand years ago, only a dozen or so humble and open-minded people were made aware of it. The rest of us had to find out about the man called Jesus from the Bible.

Jesus was known as the Christ, the Son of God. He grew up a normal little boy, but was blessed with such exceptional spiritual qualities that he outshone everyone around him. When he was thirty, his mother Mary decided he was ready to begin the ministry for which he had been born. Then, for the next three years Jesus gave the world the message their souls had been waiting to hear.

The works and teachings of Jesus can be found in the New Testament Gospels of the Bible. He created quite an impact among the ordinary folk; yet the authorities, both political and religious, were not impressed. In fact, they were so rattled by this man, who some proclaimed to be a new king for the Jewish people, that they assumed he planned to overthrow the existing religious structure.

What they didn't realise was that the man Jesus had no such intention.

As 'the king of the Jews,' Jesus was not a ruler but a leader, and the ordinary people embraced his leadership and message of hope. This they did with so much fervour that after his persecutors had him crucified, his followers covertly started up a community of faith, which eventually became known as Christianity.

Up until about the third century after his human life, the message of Jesus remained pure and reasonably intact. Then, as with everything else human beings take control of, the simplicity of the original Gospel message started to become complicated by all the variations: the rites, rituals, doctrines, and interpretations – albeit for fitting reasons at the time.

Specific terminology was formulated over the centuries that Christians were expected to understand, though only the most devout of followers really did. The Church of Rome spoke the rites in Latin, a language that few but the learned and the locals understood. Even when Christianity had spread further afield and Bible translations into the vernacular were introduced, mere mortals were left in the dark, trying to grasp the meaning of terms like 'Father, Son and Holy Ghost,' 'Sacrament' and 'Heaven.'

...What did it all mean?

And the camouflaging intensified as the centuries went by. Some branches of the faith continued to preach in Latin even though Christianity was spreading throughout the whole world. The clergy were positioned well to the front of great gothic cathedrals, creating a chasm between themselves and the rest of their congregation; thus reinforcing the separation from God instead of bringing the people closer to Him.

So going back to the first, second, or even third century before the variations began to creep in, just what was the message Jesus came to deliver?

That's easy. It was the original theme: the Kingdom of God is with us.

Now is it starting to make sense?

God must have realised that we had all lost track of our human intuition, our spiritual instincts, and that we needed help. Being a loving and forgiving benefactor, He would have been devastated that His offspring, evolved to be custodians of His special blue planet, had distanced themselves from Him. So He sent His own flesh-and-blood, spiritually speaking; to be born of a maiden who herself was pure in spirit. Then, when that child grew into an adult he would deliver a message to save his own and future generations from the devil's clutches.

As the human mother of Jesus, Mary had all the usual cares of motherhood, together with many responsibilities and graces bestowed on her in relation to the duties that her son was to perform.

The word 'Christ' raises many questions.

Jesus was not born Christ; it was not his surname, as some might think. He was born Jesus, son of Mary, but with special graces. He was perfectly in in-tune with his soul centre – his Father: God. He had a living awareness of his spirituality, and especially his God-consciousness.

At the behest of God, Jesus circulated amongst the people to assure them not only that the kingdom of God is at hand, but also to disprove the finality of death. He wanted them to know that the spirit within the human being is eternal and can conquer even that last great hurdle. Jesus did this by dying on the cross and after three days reappearing as the resurrected Christ.

He was given the title 'Christ' in respect of his oneness with God. To earn this title he demonstrated that he was no longer influenced by the allure of the devil and human conditioning, and was ready to do the work God had sent him to do.

The word 'Christ' actually means 'anointed': touched by God. This term could apply to anyone who has awakened to their spirituality and their oneness with Him. So the word 'Christ' – that is, *christ* with a small 'c' – does not relate to the human being as much as to the principle or attribute that's flowing through that human.

Imagine a battery-operated toy. The toy on its own would be nothing out of the ordinary; likewise the battery. Put them together, and the resulting device is capable of anything its maker plans for it. The human form of Jesus, together with the anointing spirit, became 'Jesus Christ.'

As a spiritual human being Jesus was able to perform miraculous feats. Yet, his message to the people implied that some of life's miracles could happen for them, too, if they abandoned their worldly ways (or sinfulness, as the Bible refers to our stubborn habits) and turned back to God. And when they did this, they could become 'christs.'

All women are called ladies, but a lady becomes a Lady with a capital 'L' when that title is bestowed on her.

Everyone can be *christed* – or, as we say, christened – but Jesus was the Christ.

Before he began His ministry, Jesus was baptised in the River Jordan by his older cousin known as John the Baptist. At the moment he was immersed in the water the voice of God was reported as saying, "This is my beloved Son in whom I am well pleased."

Although God was introducing the now grown-up Jesus, He did not suggest that Jesus was to be His only child. As a drop in the ocean of God and therefore a part of Him, each of us is also a 'child' of God in a spiritual sense. If we were ever to reach the spiritual heights of Jesus, then that voice would again be heard; this time in relation to us.

As it is, though, we're still in the process of ascending to those heights; seemingly with a long way still to go.

...But get there we will.

After all, that spiritual mountaintop is really within our souls.

We're told in the Gospels that Jesus Himself tried to put across that the king, the Messiah, was not the person but the degree of spiritual awareness within him.

He advised his followers and enquirers to 'seek you first the Kingdom of God,' informing them that his kingdom is not of this world, and assuring them that they could also attain the kingdom.

This is what's referred to as 'the pearl of great price.'

According to scripture, Jesus said, "I have overcome the world."

What do you suppose he would have meant by that – I have got the better of the world?

No, Jesus wasn't about to get the better of anybody.

It's more likely that he meant, 'I have overcome all the negative, external influences of the world and am now spiritually free. I have overcome all the worldly ways that would keep me in chains so that they no longer affect me. I am the one who *first* said, "Get thee behind me, Satan," and have risen above the devil's influence.'

When Jesus preached that 'the kingdom of God is at hand,' 'salvation is nigh,' and all the other ways in which he put his message across, he was not telling us to be good now so that when we die we'll go to Heaven. Rather, he was advising us to turn to the spiritual kingdom within our souls, and there find 'heaven' (or joy, peace and freedom) here and now, and for evermore.

We find this sort of message even in the Old Testament.

When Moses was confronted with a burning bush, he heard the voice of God say, "The place on which you stand is holy ground."

The usual interpretation of this statement is that the spot on which Moses stood was holy. But God would have been present anywhere Moses chose to stand, thereby rendering the ground holy. In this case, the word 'holy' referred as much to Moses' elevated consciousness as the ground itself.

To a lesser degree this could also relate to us: to anyone who becomes spiritually enlightened.

We think of churches as holy places. Believers allocate a specific day for the worship of God, and go to church (or its equivalent) to join with others who share their beliefs. But when you come to think of it, we don't especially need to go to a church or similar place of worship; to reserve special days, or even to think in terms of religion. For God, our life support system, is not merely in one place on one day of the week. He is everywhere on every day.

Even if we're at the office, up on the mountain with Moses, or alone in our secluded fortress, it would still be the right place and the right time for an act of worship.

Many scriptural sayings and quotations are held dear, but their real meaning is not immediately apparent. Once we become aware of the basic truth in them, such sayings come to life and take on an entirely new meaning. We take too literally what we read in the Bible and religious or philosophical books. We try to apply their ancient words to modern-day living, but in many cases this doesn't work.

That which is written in scripture is historical record. That which is written-between-the-lines within scripture is eternal truth.

We should look for the meaning behind the printed or spoken word, and apply *that* to our daily living. Today we go around in cars rather than on donkeys, but the sacred writings assure us the principles which helped the people of the biblical era will also help us if given the chance.

Although the terminology we use nowadays differs from that spoken by the writers of scripture, their old-fashioned jargon still has real meaning, which is easily understood if we apply an appropriate interpretation.

Any foreign language can be understood once the rudiments of the language have been grasped.

In a similar way, religious terminology is also easier to understand. But this can only happen when the spirit of the person who is reading the words has awoken to their intrinsic meaning.

The messages contained in stories of Christmas and Easter are examples of this.

Whatever their religious faith, people the world over acknowledge the season of Christmas. To some of us it's just an excuse to party, to some a time of giving or family gatherings, and to many it is a time of great religious importance as the feast of Jesus' birth.

However, the true significance and impact of Christmas, like many aspects of the message of Jesus, has been transformed into yet another variation.

We celebrate the birth of a child who went on to give us a life-saving message; but was it *his* message, the message of a human being?

No, it was the message of a powerful force who offered us this special little boy to bring it to the world. How else could God have got a message across to human beings but through another human being?

Jesus was, as it were, the ambassador for the country, the instrument to the musician and the dutiful Son of his Father. He was 'the pen in the hand that writes.'

So why, even now, do we make such a fuss about the historical birth of a child? It happens every day all over the world. Rather, the fuss should be made over the principle that was to be revealed through the child.

There was a seed of truth within him at the moment of his conception that would grow into the most beautiful flower of wisdom known to man. Yet, the same seed is within all human beings, too.

Rather, the Christmas we should now be celebrating is the realisation that the spiritual seeds in each of us, with the right nurturing, also have the capacity to germinate into flowers of wisdom.

All things are possible to Man – that is, *Man* with a capital 'M,' not your average human male. Jesus was Man in the highest form, and he pointed out that with the destruction of evil in our lives, all men and women can overcome the world and reclaim their spiritual identity: the Image and Likeness of God.

Christmas is an everyday occurrence, not just a once a year reminder.

In a similar way, the original significance of Easter has also been complicated.

During the hours leading up to his crucifixion Jesus, as a mere mortal, was deserted by his friends and very much alone. Just put yourself in his shoes for a moment and imagine it as though happening to you.

...Or is it already happening to you?

He was in the loneliest state of despair any human being could be in. Going through the agony of crucifixion, Jesus found it hard to believe the presence of God was still with him, or that any power could lift him up; but it did. It lifted him to the greatest heights possible and kept him there.

Even though it must have seemed otherwise while he hung on that cross, the power had not left him at all. It was just biding its time, waiting for the right moment to step forward and intervene.

Imagine a mother consoling her child who is distraught at the demise of a favourite pet. She stands by; loving, understanding and sympathising. Yet she also knows the child must suffer the anguish, that there is nothing she can or should do to stop it; and that before long the suffering will be over.

God must have also endured the anguish of knowing His beloved Son had to suffer. But it was the only way He could demonstrate His strength. Humanity would not have taken any notice otherwise.

We, too, go through our own crucifixions. Perhaps we have to. We're so out of touch with our spirituality that maybe we need to actually *fall down* the manhole in order to realise it exists.

Maybe we need to take our materialistic desires and dependencies to the limit before we finally get tired of them and begin to search for real meaning. It could be that suffering really *is* the only way we can learn by experience and become wiser for it; whether we break the law and suffer the consequences, get into drugs and find out it's not the answer or set ourselves up in a luxurious home and discover that it's no big deal after all.

It's as though God is saying to us, "I shall sit back while you drive yourselves to the limit of pain or of pleasure. I will wait until you reach a stage where you feel so trapped in the nightmare that you've got no alternative but to cry out to me – and then I'll awaken you from it!"

Maybe we need to suffer greatly before our inherited ego is driven out of us and we're able to receive our own resurrection, our own first Christmas; before our drop of water re-joins the ocean; before we can at last understand the truth and finally reach the summit of that mountain. However, we will never have to sink to those great lonely depths of turmoil that Jesus faced. He literally sweated blood as he wrestled with his anguish, for he knew he had no choice but to go through with it. He allowed himself to bear those fearful burdens to demonstrate to us that even in that hellish state; his isolated fortress – that nightmare to end all nightmares – a human being is still not alone and can still be lifted up. Who then are we to doubt such a promise?

...And wouldn't we be crazy to ignore the second chance we've been offered?

AS YOU SOW...

A basic message of the Gospels was, 'As you sow, so shall you reap.' This relates to a natural law, which is known in some circles as karmic law. Essentially, it means whatever you put into life that is what you'll get back from it.

Nowadays we're more likely to describe this law as, 'make your own bed and you have to lie in it,' and even, 'what goes around comes around.'

Anything we give of ourselves – whether love, charity and good cheer; or bitterness, selfishness and cruelty – in time it will return to us and in the same proportions as we have given it out.

Have you ever grumbled, "What have I done to deserve this?" If recently something negative has happened in your life, then the chances are you've done something which is having unpleasant repercussions for you, even if you can't remember doing anything wrong or think yourself above reproach. When I was young, my mother used to say, "Be sure your sins will find you out," and to my dismay, they always did.

Karmic law governs our basic human experience, but has nothing to do with the eternal Truth that flows through all of life. Whenever we try to achieve anything by our own efforts we break the link with our source, leaving ourselves open to this law and the possibility of failure or suffering.

An old saying tells us, 'there are no grades, rewards or punishments in nature; only consequences.'

We are therefore accountable for, and even suffer dire consequences for all our thoughts, remarks and actions. Some consequences knock us for six. Others might reveal themselves in subtle, natural and even unnoticeable ways; that is, until we begin to recognise the devil's wiles and understand what's going on. In time we can be so familiar with them that we become aware of every little effect, and are therefore in a position to influence our actions.

However, the Gospel message wasn't only, 'as you sow, so shall you reap' – make your bed and you have to lie in it; that's too final, too negative; and there was nothing final or negative about the teachings of Jesus. Also advised was, 'repent and be saved.' Renounce your worldly ways, break the influence the law of karma has had on you, by tuning in to God once more, and you will be saved from such consequences in the future.

When we give in to a force, whatever its nature, – even if we're unaware of what we're doing – we open ourselves up to negative influences and allow them to take over. Again the mind is at fault: that constantly busy part of us which is responsible for so much stress in our lives. It's the same with a phobia or obsession of any kind. Whenever we have a 'thing' about something, our minds seem to attract the negative forces that influence it.

Yet the opposite is also true. If a positive frame of mind is adopted towards even the most unlikely situation, then the picture is immediately brighter.

Another interpretation of the message is this: 'If we sow to the flesh we reap corruption; if we sow to the spirit we'll reap life everlasting.'

When we place our trust and expectation in things on a human level, then we receive on a human level – together with all the mistakes, consequences and disappointments that may be encountered as a result. Yet if instead we look to the centre of our being, or at least gaze resolutely towards the high mountain through the great religions, then we are more likely to meet with success.

In a karmic sense, we ultimately answer to no-one but ourselves. The trouble is, as we are only human; that is impatient, often arrogant and frequently fallible, we tend to think more about what's happening now or perhaps in the near future. We don't envisage what may lie around the corner, and behave impulsively without considering what the consequences might be.

Yet, the consequences are always there, and sooner or later they catch up with us.

The main effect of karmic law is to make us suffer.

Suffering appears to be a universal affliction, though at times we feel we're the only ones who *are* suffering. It involves whole nations as well as individuals; to the extent that all suffering, whether on a large or small scale, seems to be a natural result of the law of karma.

What is the worst form of suffering, anyway?

Ask a cancer sufferer and he would tell you: physical pain. Ask an infirm senior citizen and she might say: loss of independence. Ask the victims of a war-torn country and they would cite oppression, an impoverished African: hunger, a cash-strapped student: being broke, and a New Yorker: the rat race. They all experience a grinding *sense* of suffering. Only the *manner* of suffering differs.

But why do we have to suffer? We learn by suffering, of that there is no doubt. Yet so much of it exists in the world there would appear to be some deep-seated rhyme and reason behind it all. Could it be that humanity, in the many different guises that humanity takes – repressed citizen, hungry African, stressed-out American, penniless student; in other words, all of us – are now being forced to work out our karma? Are we in fact reaping what has already been sown in disobeying the universal laws?

The war-torn countries because of political intolerance; hunger on the African continent because of an imbalance within their societies; the American, the European, the rest of us, because we have turned our backs on the universal God and honour only ourselves and the power we think we possess?

Whether the effects of karmic law are on a personal scale or involve nations and creeds, how can the spell be broken?

That's simple; in principle, anyway.

Yet the reason these consequences have plagued us for so long is because those affected, out of indifference or otherwise, have neglected to revisit the time when our 'original theme' was given to humanity, and to live once more according to its laws.

And when we begin to do this...

What need is there to say more?

SAY ONE FOR ME

Throughout biblical history one means of communicating with God has been employed. Claims are frequently made as to its effectiveness, but because they are often difficult to prove, we tend to be sceptical about it.

That means of communicating is prayer.

Those unconnected with a religion may regard prayer as merely the reciting of prepared words, spoken parrot-fashion, with no real meaning for the one reciting them.

How often as children did we recite before a meal, "For what we are about to receive may the Lord make us truly thankful," without giving thought to the words we were saying?

Prayer is something we are required to take part in on specific occasions: at some school assemblies, occasionally at meetings, and generally at baptisms, weddings and funerals. It's a part of life; yet another tradition that's been handed down to us. But it doesn't really mean anything.

Right?

...No. Wrong!

Prayer recited parrot-fashion may be meaningless, but true prayer – the meditation of the heart, mind and soul; the connection with the source of our being – not only has meaning, but is also a powerful tool in the hands of the spiritually aware.

True prayer can be initiated by tuning in to your soul; or it can be brought about by extending your arms outwards and upwards to the great deity on high.

It is declared, not only by the lips, but also from the heart. It is felt within the deepest recesses of your own soul; and it may be agonised over by your emotions or sung joyfully from your spirit.

There's nothing the Creator of the universe appreciates in his children more than a 'humble and contrite heart.'

As the benefactor and Father of all, He rejoices when one of us finally turns away from the devil's allure and reaches upwards (or inwards) towards Him.

With great love He listens for – and hears – the prayers of those who have recognised their true identity and are sincerely seeking His help; even if to begin with they say, "Well, here I am, Lord. I feel a bit stupid, just sitting here talking to myself, but I believe that somehow you can sort out the mess I seem to be in. So now it's over to you."

...It's a start.

Remember, prayer is not a new concept to you now. If, while reading this book, you've begun turning inwards, then without even realising it you will have been practicing prayer.

Every time you focus your attention to seek comfort or advice, you are praying.

Whenever you have managed to lessen the ramblings of your mind and experienced peace deep within your soul, you have been meditating.

Possibly without being aware of it, you've been sending into the ethers a positive and uplifting message of hope, merely by turning to the God within and demonstrating to Him that you're ready to 'come home' again.

Nothing on the face of this planet is more effective than the power of positive prayer.

When we pray, we're communicating *with* God. When we are meditating, we contemplate *on* God.

Both these forms of prayer recharge our spiritual batteries. In rejuvenating our souls, our bodies and minds are charged with vital energy: an effect that no bottle of pills could truly achieve.

Prayer helps to solve all of our problems, answers all our questions, soothes our souls and sets us free from the forces of darkness. What's more, when the human spirit is elevated to that of the Christ-consciousness, prayer can heal the infirm and move proverbial mountains. If anything is likely to bring about the changes our world is crying out for, it is prayer.

Pray, if you will, for changes within yourself. Pray also for stability in your family. Then pray for harmony within your community, your city, your nation and your world. And when you've completely run out of things to pray for, exclaim one last great word: "AMEN!" – *SO BE IT;* for this is what 'Amen' means. That four-letter word we mumble inaudibly at the end of our prayers packs a mighty punch. It's a statement of intent, an affirmation of faith. It's like pressing 'ENTER' on your computer or 'SEND' on your mobile phone. It tells God you are bonding your will with His, your mind with His, and in doing so you are reaching out to claim your birthright as a child of God.

But don't forget also to thank Him. Any gift accepted requires a 'thank you,' does it not? And if this gift is greatly appreciated, then God would like nothing better than to hear you singing His praises, even if you are tone deaf.

"We laud and magnify your holy name, O God. We praise you for your glory and thank you for your loving kindness."

This is, in fact, God expressing Himself to His children, as His children and *through* His children. As He revitalises our souls He receives our praises: a continuous elliptical motion of which we are a vital part.

Even Jesus communicated with God through prayer. The Gospels tell us he gave his disciples a prayer they could use regularly: another of the ones we recite parrot-fashion, yet one that says it all. The prayer is commonly known as 'The Lord's Prayer,' and goes as follows:

'Our Father who art in Heaven,
Hallowed be Thy Name.
Thy Kingdom come,
Thy will be done on Earth as it is in Heaven.
Give us this day our daily bread,
And forgive us our trespasses
As we forgive those who trespass against us.
And lead us not into temptation,
But deliver us from evil.
For Thine is the Kingdom, the Power and the Glory,
Forever and ever, Amen.'

Is this prayer new to you, or have you always known it by heart?

Whichever is the case, now go back to the beginning and read it through again; only this time, read each line slowly to digest the meaning.

Do you *see* the meaning, now?

Are you, perhaps for the first time, seeing real meaning in something familiar that previously you've only glossed over? If you are, then doesn't that represent progress in your ascent of the spiritual ladder?

Say the prayer again, this time with all your heart – as a fully-fledged child of God. For if you can understand and *feel* the meaning behind the words of the Lord's Prayer, then you truly have become a child of God.

...That is, a Child with a *capital* 'C.'

AND THE GREATEST OF THESE...

Jesus is perhaps best-known for his teachings about love and forgiveness. Again, these words can seem ambiguous when you've never experienced either in your life.

Why then is forgiveness considered to be so important? What does it achieve when you say, "I forgive you," to another person? Is it said for his benefit, or for yours?

And if that person beats you or makes your life difficult, how can your forgiveness of him help to remedy or even improve the situation?

To practice forgiveness benefits the person offering it because it enables you to let go of the negativity that's upsetting your demeanour. It releases the venom of anger and helps to clear the mind. What's more, it lessens the hold that the situation requiring forgiveness has had on you, and it demonstrates to God that you're willing to make the sacrifice in the process.

So there is no doubting the benefits of being the forgive-*er*. But how will it help the forgive-*ee* – the person you're being asked to forgive?

The act of forgiveness not only releases the forgive-er from the harmful effects of his own negative thoughts, but likewise the forgive-ee once he acknowledges what he's been doing. Mind you, if he's beating you even while you're in the process of forgiving him, then it probably won't do much good. First you would need to stop him from hitting you; then you'd be in a better position to rationalise with him and eventually offer your forgiveness.

We talk about the need to implement a 'tough love' approach when it's deemed necessary. Unfortunately, in the shameless, get-away-with-anything climate of today, some of us seem to need more than the 'turn the other cheek' teachings of the New Testament. So there's no doubting assertiveness has its place in today's society.

Even strategically-aimed fury has its place, so long as it's not harboured, for that allows the devil to sneak in.

The greatest act of forgiveness was demonstrated by Jesus as he hung on the cross. "Father, forgive them; they know not what they do," is the best known translation of his words. In his last moments, he must have realised it was ignorance and pride, initiated by the devil, that drove the people to condemn him. Yet he had come among us to release those same offenders from the bondage of human conditioning.

Even in those impossible circumstances he was still able to recognise the need to save them from committing further sins. For the burden of guilt inflicted upon them would have been horrendous, had they realised what they were doing; not only for perpetuating original sin but also for killing the Son of God.

Literally, he shifted the burden of sin from them before the law of karma had time to settle it more firmly into their collective consciousness.

Christian doctrine teaches us that Jesus Christ, during his crucifixion, died to save us. This was something I couldn't understand as a child. Now I believe it to mean that Jesus, in dying, saved us from the karmic burden of guilt and sin.

It's easy to forgive someone who you know will be remorseful, and may even learn a lesson from his sins. But, forgiving in a situation where there's nothing but malicious intent on his part, can only be described as agonising. You wonder what good it can possibly achieve. Yet, forgiveness is not detectable on the surface; it acts at soul level. This means that just as Jesus exerted his intense spirituality to lift the burden of sin from those who crucified him, so in a lesser way will our forgiveness of a wrongdoer release some of the burden he's brought upon himself.

Yes, even if he doesn't know he's being forgiven and would probably resent it if he did!

True forgiveness can bring about the most important aspect of the teachings of Jesus: that of love.

Again as a child, I could not understand it when we sang the Sunday school hymn, 'Jesus loves me this I know, for the Bible tells me so.'

I remember thinking, "That's silly. I don't know any such thing. How can I be loved by something I can't even see?"

Besides, as there are so many different interpretations of the word, exactly which kind of love was Jesus supposed to be loving me with?

...I know better now.

Some people find it hard to accept the idea of love where God is concerned. To think of closeness, oneness or 'in harmony with,' seems more appropriate than 'love' for a relationship with our Maker.

To use 'love' implies there must be a subject and an object: You over there loving me over here.

In other words: separation.

But if the word also means to intensely feel love within your heart and soul, then it's the correct one to use. For that's the physical feeling we receive when the channels between the human and the divine are flung open, and a glow 'warms the cockles of the heart.' Known in some circles as 'the Sacred Heart of Jesus,' it's this application of the word 'love' that better relates to the love of Jesus for humankind – and, so I later learnt, for me as well.

As a tightly-folded bud bursts open when stimulated by the 'love' of nature, so do our hearts burst open with the love we receive from God; whether directly within our souls or through Jesus and the other historic masters of religion. What greater love could there be than to ignite the spiritual centre in mankind?

And not just the activity of God in man, but also that of people with one another: the love of God working in us and through us.

The essence of life throughout the ages has been the golden thread of love.

We love one another so differently; from our concern for someone in distress to the passion between two lovers. Yet all come under the heading of the word 'love.'

The degree to which we feel love is dictated by our emotions, but the spark deep down inside, that seems at times to set our souls on fire, is instilled in us and we have no control over it.

We don't choose to love or care for one person and not the next; it just happens that way. And when it does, love can do some peculiar things to us; things of which we would otherwise think ourselves incapable. Have you ever fallen in love and found that you can't eat or sleep; that you can't keep your mind on your job and have trouble rationalising? Such feelings are uncontrollable because they aren't put there by us – or rather, by our minds and emotions. They come from a source within that's much deeper than these superficial feelings. They come from soul.

...And what is soul, but God?

The love of human beings, one for the other: this is what Jesus wanted when he said, "Love thy neighbour." This, and the love of man for the world we live in, is God expressing Himself as you and me, for you and me, and through you and me.

The love of God expresses itself through us in so many ways: as the complexities of physical form and as caring for those in need; as talent to enrich our lives, the capacity to appreciate the qualities of a rose, and the inspiration behind thought and creation.

As we collectively progress up our spiritual ladder, so is God ever more joyfully able to express Himself through us to the rest of humanity; until one day...

Is peace on Earth such an elusive dream?

A MOVE IS AFOOT

The biblical messages of love and forgiveness have been an important part of spiritual teachings for two thousand years now. As a consequence of this, humankind has made worthy spiritual progress.

In general, the nations of the world are more accepting of each other than in previous centuries; although areas of unrest still exist due to the constant infiltration of negative forces, and to our separation from the internal spirit.

However, progress has been gradual. In fact, throughout the course of history it's been so gradual we might not have realised it was taking place.

Think for a moment, though, about the knowledge you may have of the history behind our Western civilisation. Let's take certain points in history and compare them. For instance, think back to the days of Moses with the cycle of slavery and the plagues; to the time of Jesus when the brutal Roman Empire reigned supreme. Think ahead a millennium or so to the reign of Henry VIII or the Industrial Revolution, when life in developed countries was more civilised but nevertheless still harsh. And then, advance in your thinking to the last century, which saw at its onset the final abolition of slavery, women's suffrage and the rise of commercial might; and ended with improvement in the field of medicine, global communication and travel, and a general opening up of culture to the world by way of the Internet.

Even though, during each of those past eras, conditions in themselves were often grim, don't you see that since the early days of Moses there has been some kind of upward movement in humanity? People have generally become more aware of each other; more natural and sincere. We have been learning by experience and moving up the spiritual ladder, even though humanity itself might not be conscious of the fact. We are gradually leaving behind those early days when humans thought they didn't need their source of life; when under the law of karma and attracted by the glitter of evil, mankind brought about 'the Fall' for himself and ensuing generations.

Yet, throughout all of this time, the Father Figure has been watching over these detached souls. Whenever an opening has presented itself, He has responded to prayer and provided guidelines to help them along. He rushed in through prophets of ancient and more modern times, and He sent us Jesus.

In Moses' time He helped the people by giving Moses a set of standards to guide them on their journey through the desert and through life. We've come to know them as 'the Ten Commandments,' and still regard them as God's rules and regulations; but consider this:

Doubtless these commandments did come directly from God. However, it's also possible that the last eight of the commandments – which were basically, 'thou shalt not kill, steal, covet, commit adultery, worship idols, bear false witness, honour father and mother, and keep the Sabbath day' – may well have concerned karmic law. Looking at it from that perspective, they seem to be not so much rules as guidelines. They would have been given in order to free wayward people from karma and sinful living, and to help them reap a better life on a human level; in other words, to 'repent and be saved.'

Surely, the only real *laws* that God has for us are to 'love the Lord thy God and Him only shalt thou serve,' and to 'love thy neighbour as thyself.' The first of these deals with our original theme; the second one is already being adopted throughout the world by natural choice. With and even *without* religious connections, humankind as a whole is moving up the spiritual ladder.

Really, there's no such thing as 'sin;' certainly not in the traditional sense of the word. There is only wrong-doing in the shape of error, misunderstanding and bad judgment; of our being blinded by the forces of evil and not knowing any better; of not knowing what to do, and therefore not able to take control of our lives. So there is no grievous sin to be atoned for, but merely a condition to be improved upon, an ignorance to be educated, an understanding to be developed and a wrong to be forgiven.

People's attitudes towards each other in Moses' day were merciless; not because they were bad, but because they didn't know any better. They had allowed themselves to adopt trends that were considered unacceptable in a spiritual sense, therefore attracting bad karma. So those commandments were necessary at the time.

During the time of Jesus, attitudes had improved, but still left much to be desired. He taught in his distinctive style, the Sermon on the Mount in particular, to assist the people of that era, and also as a guide for those in the centuries to come.

Over the last couple of millennia, our way of thinking and behaviour in general have progressed even further. Nowadays a great many people have already attained the state of mind whereby they do 'love their neighbour as themselves.' So the basic message has been the same right from the start; no matter in what form it was presented or during which era.

Just think: if someone like Moses lived in the here and now, what would his commandments be? The imagination runs wild. Perhaps they would include: 'thou shalt not pollute our lovely planet; thou shalt treat all people with equality; thou shalt not create or destroy unwanted life.' Or how about, 'thou shalt not mug thy neighbour!'

These days, many activities – political, business, sporting and cultural – are designed to bring people together. As individuals we've begun to recognise the need to love, to share and to unite. We can see clearly, more so now than in any century before us, that deep down we are really no different from anyone else in the world. More importantly, we see the same realisation in each other.

When countries unite in sporting fixtures such as a World Cup series or the Olympic Games, the emphasis as shown on television is usually that of human achievement: on who has secured the Cup or how many gold medals have been won. Yet the real significance of these events goes deeper than that. It is the coming together of human souls as one integrated community. Imagine it: two thirds of the world's population tuned in 'live' to an Olympic opening ceremony. Then, at the closing ceremonies all the cultural barriers disappear and the athletes mingle as one; as members of a greater humanity, just as the spirit of God intended.

A similar unifying situation occurs in time of strife. In wartime, natural disasters, civil and family emergencies – even during trade-union unrest – the people involved rally round and give support unselfishly; perhaps for the first or only time in their lives. Then there's national pride, and the patronage that's offered unconditionally for cultural events or political rallies.

The individual 'ego' recedes into the background. For the duration of the event something more profound comes to the fore; to unite with the same 'something' in everyone else.

Even when nothing visibly occurs to suggest unification, there is still spiritual activity covertly taking place: unseen beneath the surface.

During World War II, conditions within France were atrocious and to all appearances there seemed to be little hope for the survival of the nation. But it did survive – with support and the gallant efforts of the French Resistance. Their activities were never visible on the surface, yet their underground movement was ever-present when needed; stealthily acting out a role that helped to bring about the salvation of their country.

And so it is with the spiritual salvation of our world. There may be no sign on the surface that the spirit is at work. We're so accustomed to seeing the gloomy aspects of life that we tend to forget there's also a brighter side.

But an underground movement is continuously present; stealthily working on our behalf.

It may seem to be taking a long time for changes to become obvious, but humanity is dealing in millennia. Our history spans many centuries and generations; not merely years or decades. Whether we're consciously aware of it or not, there's definitely a move afoot to bring this human race of ours into a sense of oneness, growth and reality, if we will let it.

...I say again: "If we will let it."

As thinking human beings, all we seem to do is create turmoil; so it's not human will that achieves the unifying.

Rather, it's the underground movement; the spirit of God flowing through humanity, that brings about the changes.

It's the spirit of God in each of us that colours our jigsaw pieces. It motivates us to invent the mobile phone, shows us how to bounce live pictures around the world; to make a plane travel faster than the speed of sound, create a worldwide computer network, and think up a way of involving all the sporting nations of the world in one great happening; or just to bring a little joy into someone else's life. And as with all of God's creations, even though we may not be aware of it, He is watching over our every activity.

You may be tempted to ask, "But what about all the trouble that's present in the world today? We're slipping towards oblivion, not progressing."

Yes, it does look like that at times. On occasions the devil does appear to be gaining the upper hand.

When these feelings overwhelm you, remind yourself of the underground movement: the spirit that works in and through enlightened people around the world. As others come to recognise the source of their inspiration, so this movement will flourish. But it can only be achieved in the conscious awareness of every one of us; even if we must struggle in order to make progress.

Yet, who's to say that despite the law of karma there isn't also some good, some real purpose to the terrible things that have happened, and that are still happening around the world? Haven't we learnt some almighty lessons from mistakes we and our predecessors have made?

If there wasn't once slavery, would the world have been shocked into recognising the cruelty of enslaving another human being? Without the activities of Greenpeace would we be as conservation conscious as we are now? If the atomic bombs were not released over Japan, would the knowledge that we can never engage in nuclear war be as absolute as it is today?

Isn't it a fact that even on a small scale, it takes tragedy or mishap to knock some sense into us, and that our individual, most minor trials and tribulations often result in a lesson well learnt?

So look a little deeper at the world around you. Draw your attention outside the walls of your fortress and regard everything from a fresh perspective. Take a closer look at the ordinary everyday things that we take so much for granted. Think about the aspect of life that matters most in the world: that which goes on in the heart, mind and soul of all individuals who have the spirit of life flowing through them.

This is not their appearance – the fanatical, the sullen, the arrogant; the colour, the race, the creed – but what lies beneath. We judge by what we see, yet that's only superficial: the tip of the iceberg.

...Look beneath.

During a drought the grass seems to be devoid of life, and to all appearances is no longer capable of growth. But what happens when it rains?

The truth, the life and the growth lie beneath what you can see.

Look beneath and pray for spiritual rain; for it will come in time.

UNIVERSAL GATHERING

The spiritual future for our own lives, and for the world we live in, could be extremely positive if we allowed it to be.

Sometimes, though, we have to question what there is to be positive about; for there's no denying some of the horrors that are taking place, both personally and around the globe. Anyone with a degree of sensitivity must at times feel overcome with a sense of hopelessness by all that we hear in the news.

Yet, there are also some wonderful things going on. For instance, it wouldn't be broadcast on the six o'clock news that a young woman across town, diagnosed with cancer, had such a strong faith in God that He answered both her prayers and those of her faith community, and now all traces of her cancer have disappeared. However, it would be splashed across the front page of the 'Morning Herald' if researchers from across town found an actual cure for the disease.

There is plenty going on to gladden our hearts which is never reported upon, either locally or virally, because the stories, although wonderful for the people concerned, are not considered newsworthy.

Spend a moment or two inside an empty church, temple, mosque or synagogue. Drink in the peacefulness of this healing environment and then try to tell the local tabloid how you feel. They wouldn't waste a second on it. Now, if you told them that you and others witnessed an apparition of the Archangel Michael or the prophet Elijah while you were at prayer and had cellphone pictures to prove it, they might be interested.

The subtle activities of God go unnoticed by all except those who are on the receiving end. And like any other underground movement, these activities are still going on even though they're seldom broadcast around the world.

You don't need to belong to an organised religion to have a relationship with God, but it helps. When you've grasped the meaning of terminology you may once have called 'religious gobbledygook,' the real advantages of belonging to a faith community become clear.

For one thing, you will find companionship. If you're lonely, there's nothing better to bring warmth to your heart than a cheery welcome when you attend a service or meeting. The family atmosphere within a faith community is born of spirit but demonstrated in its friendship towards all those who come within reach.

Then there's the opportunity to focus. When you are daily rushed off your feet, to have an excuse – or grasp the opportunity – to take time out and come together with others who share your beliefs, both benefits the soul and gives you something to look forward to; not forgetting the peace and uplift experienced during worship.

And lastly, there's the sense of security that belonging to a faith community brings. There will always be evil in the world, waiting to get its hooks into you and drag you down again. As part of a religious community you are protected both humanly and spiritually, which brings with it a wonderful sense of security.

Jesus himself assured us that where two or more of us are gathered in his name, there he will also be. No demons can penetrate the aura surrounding a group of awakened human souls.

They say that the great religions survived the ravages of time for two reasons: The accounts of their founders' lives are historically authentic, and because the believers who passed on the teachings formed strong faith communities down through the ages.

My own faith community is Catholic.

The word 'catholic' actually means 'universal.'

It's a term that could apply to any one of the world's great religions. Think of the implications:

A universal gathering: One family in spirit throughout the whole world, regardless of national and international borders. Each branch of the family is supported by the spirituality of its leaders and members. Their purpose is to love and serve a Creator who is both at the centre of their own being and encompassing the entire globe.

That's what religion in general is really all about.

...Or at least, it should be.

Does this picture appear a little too idealistic to be true these days? If so, why?

Could it be because those who currently make up the family of God still worship the deity on the high mountain but not the divinity within their souls?

When I was young, my family belonged to a strong faith community in Great Britain. I was baptised into it, grew up in it and involved myself in many areas of church life well into adulthood. Then I married and we moved to the other side of the world.

Soon afterwards, I became aware of something I could not have foreseen: there was now a great void in me. Without ever suspecting it could happen, on leaving my homeland I also left behind every aspect of my church life. Even though I joined a new community where we went to live, it was not the same; and for this reason:

While I attended the church of my youth, I often took part in the diverse activities of the church, but overlooked my intrinsic spirituality.

Then after we left, I realised that my relationship had only been with the community, and not with God. I didn't even discover until some years later that I possessed a spiritual centre. The God of my younger days had always been separate and apart from me: on that distant peak. So when I detached from my church, I also lost my perception of God.

The experience of being plunged into the void took its toll. They call it, 'the dark night of the soul.'

It wasn't until my soul received a jolt – during a casual conversation with a janitor, no less – that I awoke from the nightmare. All he did was inform me that God's spirit flows through *me* as well as through the rest of the universe.

Almost instantaneously I woke up from the nightmare and discovered my soul centre, the hub of my being. The walls of my fortress came down and revealed the world as it really is. Then I was in a position to relate the 'wheel' to the 'mountain,' and view my early experience of religion from a better perspective.

I now believe this to be the problem with a traditional approach to religion, and the reason why the number of attendees for some religions is falling.

As long as people assume God to be merely at the top of the mountain, religion has little attraction, because the idea of a distant God holds no meaning.

To make matters worse, only a proportion of believers who attend a place of worship actually communicate with the God within their souls. Others have not yet grasped that this is where we must first seek Him.

As I discovered from my youth, there is a big difference between social religion and spiritual religion.

Going to church out of habit or because it was expected of me, did not benefit my soul and, spiritually speaking, was practiced for all the wrong reasons. Now I go to my place of worship to focus on God, to mix with others who are in touch with the reality of it all, and for the intrinsic security of a universal family.

Unfortunately, there is also another stumbling block in the way of spiritual understanding: the religious intolerance that's still rife, even today.

The traditional religions tend to regard faith only from their own viewpoint. They don't take into account the universal or global picture of spirituality. Yet the picture is incomplete without each religion also acknowledging the beliefs of other faiths.

Imagine you were to paint a portrait of someone you loved. You would no doubt concentrate your efforts on the subject. This might be the most beautiful face in the world, retaining the interest of the onlooker without any need of further adornment.

Yet, even though the portrait may be perfect in itself, the painting cannot be deemed complete until its setting – the background décor or landscape – has been included.

This is what has happened with our religious affiliations. We concentrate only on the 'face' of our own faith: the image of God on the mountain top, or the teachings of our own spiritual mentor. Instead, we should really take into account the universal setting that gives religion a more complete expression of spirituality.

As the saying goes, 'There are many pathways up the mountain, yet the view from the top is still the same.'

Certain religions have inherited stigma down the centuries and on into the present.

Firstly, at intervals there have been corrupt practices by their human members that were wrongly attributed to the actual religions.

Secondly, religious reformists who themselves rejected the notion of an internal God, sought redress by enforcing changes to match their own way of thinking.

Nevertheless, corruption aside, religion is still a direct and ever present link with God.

Referring back to Christianity for a moment, did you know there's an unbroken chain that dates back to the time of Jesus?

It began when he handed the mantle of authority for founding his church to his disciple Peter. After that, as the centuries rolled by and a recognised, established church came into being, that same authority was handed down through sacred rite from one leader of the faith to the next.

To me, the concept of a direct lineage dating back two whole millennia is both mind-blowing and comforting. It reaches out and touches me in the here and now through the ordained leader of my own faith community. Then the leader, in extending his arms over the people, blesses them with the same ongoing spirit.

Depending on how you look at this kind of thing, it's either something special or completely meaningless. But when you are feeling pretty empty to begin with, the devil makes sure you regard most things as meaningless, don't you think?

In actual fact, it's rather wonderful – continuous chains of spirituality throughout the world, which even today link us to the founders of ancient yet still-living faiths. And this, also enhancing the fact that the same spirit is found within the depths of the human heart.

Even if you choose to 'go it alone' in your relationship with God, you can still have it all.

Each of us, whether we're layman or clergy – including our own Pontiff – at some stage has to be alone.

Every day we still have to go back home, to our own selves and our private thoughts; to the long, often lonely nights when we have only our minds for company, when our spiritual journey is a solitary exercise. So you need not belong to an established religion in order to maintain a personal relationship with God.

Yet it can be a wild and wicked world without spiritual security, and these days the term 'safety in numbers' is more appropriate for this than you can image.

Whichever way you choose to go, you'll be embarking on a brand new journey, a journey full of hope and excitement; for you will recognise that at long last you've awoken from the nightmare.

You will have been delivered from the darkness of your fortress into the light of spiritual freedom.

On looking back, you will realise that such freedom is indeed ours for the asking.

After years of being immersed in the nightmare, it is a wondrous thing to wake up and discover the truth about ourselves and about life in general; a truth that's both simple and effective.

This is what gives us real freedom – spiritual freedom.

The sun is still shining; even though where you live it may be the middle of the night. There is absolutely no reason to doubt it, so why doubt the power behind it?

The greatest gift in the world is the gift of yourself – your Self and your God – and these you already possess deep within you.

So just relax, be yourself and feel free.

...You *are* free – in the greatest sense of the word.

www.ingramcontent.com/pod-product-compliance
Lightning Source LLC
Chambersburg PA
CBHW061301110426
42742CB00012BA/2014